Konjaku Monogatari-shū

Twayne's World Authors Series

Roy E. Teele, Editor
University of Texas, Austin

TWAS 621

Photograph courtesy of Professor Mori Masato, Aichi Prefectural University, Nagoya, Japan, who owns the manuscript.

Konjaku Monogatari-shū

By W. Michael Kelsey

Nanzan University
Nagoya, Japan

Twayne Publishers • Boston

Konjaku Monogatari-shū

W. Michael Kelsey

Copyright © 1982 by G. K. Hall & Co.
All Rights Reserved
Published by Twayne Publishers
A Division of G. K. Hall & Company
70 Lincoln Street
Boston, Massachusetts 02111

Book production by Marne B. Sultz
Book design by Barbara Anderson

Printed on permanent/durable acid-free
paper and bound in the United States of
America.

Library of Congress Cataloging in Publication Data

Kelsey, W. Michael, 1945–
    Konjaku monogatari-shū

    (Twayne's world authors series; TWAS 621)
    Bibliography: p. 166
    Includes index.
    1. Konjaku monogatari.   2. Folk literature, Japanese—
History and criticism.   3. Japanese literature—Heian
period, 794–1185—History and criticism.   4. Folk
literature, Japanese—Translations into English.
5. Folk literature, English—Translations from Japanese.
I. Title   II. Series.
PL787.K63K4   398.2′0952   82–2914
ISBN 0–8057–6463–1   AACR2

To My Mother
For Her Seventieth Birthday

Contents

About the Author
Preface
Acknowledgments
Chronology

Chapter One
The Compiler and His Times   *1*

Chapter Two
Konjaku Monogatari-shū in the *Setsuwa* Tradition   *18*

Chapter Three
The Compiler's Vision   *55*

Chapter Four
Konjaku Monogatari-shū in Japanese Literature   *99*

Chapter Five
A Critical Overview   *139*

Notes and References   *159*
Selected Bibliography   *166*
Index   *170*

About the Author

W. Michael Kelsey was born March 29, 1945. He received the A.B. in English and the Ph.D. in classical Japanese literature, with a minor in folklore, from Indiana University. His Ph.D. dissertation was on *Konjaku Monogatari-shū* as didactic literature. He has taught at Southern Illinois University at Carbondale and at Carleton College in Northfield, Minnesota; he is currently a member of the faculty of Nanzan University in Nagoya, Japan, where he teaches Japanese literature, folklore, and English. He is editorial assistant for *Asian Folklore Studies* and the *Japanese Journal of Religious Studies*.

Professor Kelsey has lived and studied in Japan for several years. He was an exchange student at Tenri University in Tenri, Japan, and was a Japan Foundation Fellow at Nanzan University. He has published articles on various topics concerning Japanese literature and mythology and is now working on a book on Japanese mythology.

Preface

Japan of the early twelfth century was a country in the midst of chaotic social, political, and economic change. The lavish aristocratic court depicted in literary works such as *The Tale of Genji* had passed through its heyday and was on the decline. Murder, rape, and theft were becoming more frequent and the aristocracy found itself powerless to maintain isolation from the depressingly mundane realities of everyday life. With increasing regularity the aristocrats found it necessary to rely on the protection of countrified warrior clans.

As their shining world grew tarnished the nobility quite understandably began to seek lasting values in creeds which promised redemption in the next life and survival in this one. Buddhism flourished, but this was a different Buddhism from that which had been popular just a hundred years earlier. Instead of stressing the glories of the present life it sang praises of Amida's Western Paradise, a place to which the faithful aspired to be reborn so that they might be able to attain full enlightenment later. But in addition to this promise for the future, late Heian Buddhism offered its followers a powerful set of weapons—among them the Lotus Sutra and the Bodhisattva—which could be used to protect oneself in this imperfect world.

From this background comes one of the world's largest collections of tales, *Konjaku Monogatari-shū* [A Collection of Tales of Long Ago]. Put together about 1100, this collection of stories—1,039 of which are still extant—offers its readers a blueprint for success, both in this world and the next. We will probably never know the identity of its compiler, though it is fairly obvious that he was a Buddhist monk and that the stories he gathered were intended for use in preaching by other monks. It is also apparent that he was concerned with both the spiritual and physical well-being of his audience, for he offers advice in both areas.

He was widely read in Buddhist literature: his collection uses stories previously published in a large number of Chinese works, including sutras, commentaries on sutras, and story collections. *Konjaku* begins with five volumes of tales set in India and concerned mostly with the life and times of the historical Buddha, then has five volumes of stories set in China which deal with both Buddhist and secular topics, and then goes on to Japan. There are ten volumes of tales on Japanese Buddhist themes and another eleven of Japanese secular tales. Three of these thirty-one volumes are no longer extant.

The sheer bulk of *Konjaku Monogatari-shū* makes it a difficult collection to deal with in any kind of perspective. *Konjaku* has appealed in different ways to different people, and the danger of oversimplifying it according to one's individual image is always present. I hope I have avoided that danger in this book, but I should warn the reader that the fact that I see *Konjaku* primarily as a religious collection compiled largely to aid in the salvation of its readers is bound to have influenced my judgment of it in places.

The purpose of this book is to introduce the reader to *Konjaku Monogatari-shū* by describing the collection and showing how it fits into the overall pattern of Japanese literature. I begin with a consideration of the compiler and his times, then attempt to locate *Konjaku* within its genre, that of *setsuwa* literature. This is followed by a discussion of the contents of the collection, which I make largely on the basis of translations of "sample" tales from each of the four major sections of the collection.

After having acquainted the reader with the basic information about the collection—its historical background, its literary tradition, and its contents—I go on to discuss it in terms of the overall picture of Japanese literature. Finally, I have attempted to give some understanding of *Konjaku* from a critical perspective, to show what makes it come alive as a work of literature.

The reader will soon notice that I spend considerably more space in discussions of the Japanese stories than of the stories from India and China. This is not because the Indian and Chinese tales are necessarily less interesting or have less literary merit than the Japanese tales (though many have assumed this to be so), nor is it because they offer no challenges to the scholar. Indeed, the Indian and Chinese tales present many fascinating scholarly problems but these are, in my opinion, best dealt with by the specialist and are not appropriate to a general introduction aimed at an audience of nonspecialists. The Japanese tales are more immediately a part of the Japanese folklore and literary traditions, and I have accordingly concentrated on them. For similar reasons I have not treated the "Chinese connection," that is, Chinese tale collections or Buddhist preaching, although these, too, might legitimately be included in a book on *Konjaku*. My concern has been mainly to examine *Konjaku Monogatari-shū* as a part of the Japanese literary tradition and not to explore the very real Chinese influence on its development.

Another area I have avoided is the whole field of linguistic studies of *Konjaku*. This lies outside my own expertise and is, moreover, difficult to communicate clearly to readers who have no understanding of classical Japanese.

A few words about mechanics. In order to avoid an excess of unnecessary footnotes I have identified passages quoted from *Konjaku* within the text, referring to the volume and story number in Roman and Arabic numerals respectively. Hence, the fourth story of the third volume would be identified as III.4.

All quotations from Japanese sources are my own work; even though often excellent English translations exist, I have found it convenient to maintain consistency in translation style so that comparisons can be more easily made between different versions of the same story. In the case of translations from *Konjaku*, my source has always been the *Nihon Koten Bungaku Taikei* version, edited by Yamada Yoshio. Japanese names have been given in the traditional Japanese order, with the family name first, then the given name.

Konjaku studies are of some importance in Japan and it is regrettable that they have barely progressed in this country. If this book inspires even one student to read any of the tales in

Konjaku and to do some thinking about the collection, it will have served its purpose. It was the individual stories in *Konjaku Monogatari-shū* which attracted me to the collection originally, and it is to the elucidation of these stories and the collection which they comprise that I have dedicated my effort in this book.

W. Michael Kelsey

Nanzan University
Nagoya, Japan

Acknowledgments

This book could never have been written without the stimulating research of a large group of Japanese scholars which underlies it. My debt to the published work of Nishio Kōichi, Kunisaki Fumimaro, and Kurosawa Kōzō, in particular, is immense, and I often feel that, try as I may, I will never attain the breadth of knowledge that they display in their work. Professors Nishio and Kunisaki, I would add, have given me much encouragement personally as well as providing me with ideas and information through the printed page—they have fed me, listened to me, and answered my questions; Professor Kunisaki even went so far as to present me with a personal copy of his book when I was unable to find it in any bookstore.

Professor Minobe Shigekatsu of Nanzan University in Nagoya is the person who first introduced me to the study of *setsuwa* and *Konjaku Monogatari-shū,* and for the past ten years he has unselfishly taught me more than either of us will ever fully know. Professor Marian Ury of the University of California, Davis, has been another source of inspiration in the seven or eight years we have been communicating on *Konjaku* and other matters. To her I also owe an immeasurable debt of gratitude. My advisor at Indiana University, Professor Kenneth Yasuda, has also contributed to my understanding of Japanese literature, and I hope it will not prove an embarrassment to him if I say that his insights into Japanese poetry are what stimulated my own interest in it.

A former colleague at Carleton College, Ulf Zimmermann, read a first draft of this book and made many valuable suggestions, for which I remain grateful. I also owe a large debt of gratitude to my editor, Roy E. Teele, both for his patience and for suggestions which have resulted in a much-improved final product.

Finally, I wish to thank Indiana University and Tenri University, which provided the financial assistance that allowed me to travel to Japan in 1970, where I was able to begin the research which culminated in this book, and Carleton College, which was generous in its support of the production of the manuscript.

Chronology

The following is a chronological listing of works mentioned in the text.

712	*Kojiki*
720	*Nihon Shoki*
821(?)	*Nihon Ryōiki*
900(?)	*Taketori Monogatari*
905	*Kokin Waka Shū*
935	*Tosa Nikki*
950(?)	*Yamato Monogatari; Ise Monogatari*
963	*Kagerō Nikki*
980	*Utsubo Monogatari*
984	*Sambō E Kotoba*
985	*Ōjō Yōshū*
986	*Nihon Ōjō Gokuraku Ki*
1007	*Izumi Shikibu Nikki*
1011	*Genji Monogatari*
1035	*Eiga Monogatari*
1040–43	*Dai Nihon Hokke Genki*
1060	*Sarashina Nikki*
1094	*Fusō Ryakki*
1100(?)	*Konjaku Monogatari-shū*
1110(?)	*Hyakuza Hōdan Kikigaki-shō*
1126–31(?)	*Kohon Setsuwa Shū*
1129	*Ōkagami*

1134	*Uchigiki-shū*
1170	*Ima Kagami*
1190(?)	*Senjūshō*
1195	*Mizu Kagami*
1202	*Mumyō Zōshi*
1212	*Hōjōki*
1215	*Hosshin-shū*
1220	*Hōgen Monogatari; Heiji Monogatari*
1221(?)	*Uji Shūi Monogatari*
1222	*Kankyo no Tomo*
1242(?)	*Heike Monogatari*

Chapter One

The Compiler and His Times

Konjaku Monogatari-shū is the largest and best-known collection of those short tales which are known in Japan as *setsuwa*. A vast, sprawling work, *Konjaku* contains 1,039 extant stories in its twenty-eight volumes (three other volumes have been lost), and has been the subject of a considerable amount of attention from both scholars and writers since it was put together by an unknown compiler about 1100.

Most of the key questions concerning this work remain to be resolved. The identity of its compiler is still unknown, as are the exact circumstances under which it was compiled. Its date is a matter of debate and we are not even sure about its proper name. Approaching a collection so large with such a diverse selection of stories one feels an affinity with the plight of the blind men who attempted to define the elephant. It is far too easy to seize one part of the whole and magnify the work into an imaginative distortion of our incomplete understanding.

In this book I shall introduce *Konjaku* and some of the more important views of it to the Western reader. This task is made somewhat more difficult by the fact that accomplishing it requires a multifaceted approach. One cannot discuss the stories themselves, for example, without some knowledge of the compiler and his times, but any discussion of the identity of the compiler must rest on a reading of the individual tales. Obviously, it is impossible to carry on these discussions simultaneously, so I will present here the briefest of introductions to *Konjaku* before moving on to a more detailed treatment of the compiler; the reader will find that many of the points which appear to be only vaguely supported in this chapter will be picked up again in the third chapter, where I will deal more thoroughly with the contents of the collection.

Konjaku Monogatari-shū is an encyclopedic work which was compiled primarily for the betterment—both spiritual and social—of its audience. Its main thrust is Buddhist, and two-thirds of its tales are directly concerned with Buddhism. Compiled as it was in one of the least stable periods of Japanese history, it is not difficult to understand the need felt by the author to provide his audience with a blueprint for life. The set of plans he offers for success in the world comes from a Buddhist master craftsman, but the collection contains a good number of stories labeled "secular," and these stories address the more secular needs of the audience.

The original thirty-one volumes (VIII, XVIII, and XXI are no longer extant) are organized geographically. Volumes I–V contain stories set in India, VI–X contain stories set in China, and XI–XXXI contain stories set in Japan. Within the Chinese tales, Volume X features secular stories; the Japanese secular stories are to be found in volumes XXI–XXXI. There are other levels of organization to be found in *Konjaku,* however, both in the overall collection and within the individual volumes, and the work does have a general unity despite the fact that it is composed of so many different types of tales.

The person who masterminded this collection was an unknown compiler. It is unlikely that we will ever know this person's exact identity, or the year in which his task was completed. Thousands of words have been written on these topics, and a considerable amount of scholarly blood has been shed in the pages of learned journals, but the conclusion remains the same: in the absence of any new evidence the exact identity of the compiler and the date of compilation must remain unknown.

From the morass of scholarly debate, however, two facts stand out which seem to be self-evident and indisputable. These are that *Konjaku* was compiled during a period of major social and political change in Japan and that it was compiled by a Buddhist monk. The second of these facts has not always been accepted by scholars, for the authorship of *Konjaku* has been traditionally attributed to an aristocrat. Few would dispute the first, however.

The stories in *Konjaku* constitute the best evidence for the conclusion that the collection was made in a time of confusion and social instability. They abound in descriptions of thefts, rapes and murders, and the compiler frequently reminds us just how bad the times are. That his answers to the problems of the times are usually Buddhist and that he has organized his collection along Buddhist lines convince me that he himself was a Buddhist monk.

In any examination of the identity of the compiler, then, it is necessary to consider the times in which he was living, and in what follows I will present a brief discussion of the social and religious history of the period during which *Konjaku* was written. I shall then discuss the traditional theory and some more recent theories as to who the compiler might have been.

Heian Buddhism, the *Insei* Period, and *Konjaku*

The Heian period (794–1185) is generally classified as a time of aristocratic dominance of the politics and society of Japan. This is certainly true, but it is also true that the position of the aristocrats eroded steadily, and that by the time *Konjaku* was compiled the aristocracy had lost much of the glory it had had in, say, the early tenth century. This is not the place to present a full history of the Heian period, but I would like to outline the major trends here so that we may have a better picture of the times and a better understanding of the nature of Heian Buddhism.[1]

When the move to Heian (present day Kyoto) was made from Nara in 794 the position of the emperor was perhaps as secure as it has ever been in the history of Japan. As time passed, however, the imperial family fell under the domination of a branch of the Fujiwara family; this control was exercised largely through the continued marriage of Fujiwara women to emperors. The emperors were often forced to abdicate early and a Fujiwara regent would then speak for the new child emperor. Some of these regents also served as directors of the civil government and had nearly absolute power.

In 1068, however, the Emperor Go-Sanjō, the first sovereign in nearly two hundred years who was not under the control of the Fujiwara family, took steps to increase the power of his own clan. His example was followed by his son, Shirakawa, who officially abdicated in 1086 but continued to rule from his position in retirement. This state of affairs continued until Taira Kiyomori, the head of a warrior clan, took control of the state in 1179, placing the retired Emperor Go-Shirakawa under house arrest.

The Heian period is thus one which first saw a shift from imperial authority to aristocratic authority, then saw the breakup of aristocratic authority and eventual domination by the military classes. The aristocracy continued to control the cultural life of the country, but its members were forced to watch as their political and economic power faded away. The military eventually took control of the country in 1185 with the founding of the Kamakura shogunate. The period from about 1068 to the end of the Heian period in 1185, one of transition and instability, is usually called the *insei* period, or the time of government by retired emperors. Diaries from the times contain numerous references to various sorts of disasters and criminal acts, and the tales of *Konjaku Monogatari-shū* reflect the grim social realities of the times. One might say that the *Konjaku* compiler was balanced precariously between the chrysanthemum and the sword; certainly he was aware that he was living in an uncertain age.

Buddhism, as one might expect, reflected many of these social realities and changed along with the political and economic structures. We find two strong and seemingly incompatible tendencies in Heian Buddhism, especially during the strife-ridden twelfth century. The first of these is a tendency to be world affirming and to embrace the values of this life fully, while the other is a tendency to deny the world and place emphasis on the life to come. This latter trend gave rise to what is often referred to as the "new" Buddhism of the Kamakura period.

To understand the presence of these two aspects of Heian Buddhism it is necessary to consider briefly the early nature of this religion in Japan. Buddhism was originally foreign to Japan, and spread from the top levels of society down to the lower classes. This popularization was a long time in maturing and it might be argued that it was only in the Kamakura period that Buddhism began to speak to the needs of the people, though this is a considerably oversimplified stance to take. In any event, Buddhism was first the property of the emperor, who used it for his own purposes, as it was considered to be a religion of great magical power. Strict regulations were written for monks and nuns, largely to keep this powerful religion out of the hands of the wrong people.

This was the beginning of the world affirming aspect of Heian Buddhism—it was first used to help maintain the status quo. As the nature of the state began to change, however, so too did the nature of Buddhism. When the capital was moved to Heian two major sects were formed. These are Tendai, founded by Saichō (762–822; he is also known as Dengyō Daishi, a posthumous title), and Shingon, founded by Kūkai (774–835; he is also known as Kōbō Daishi). Tendai is the more universal sect of the two, and embraced nearly all of the major practices of its day, including the worship of the Lotus Sutra and faith in Amida and his Western Paradise. Shingon is an esoteric Buddhism, given to secret teachings and the use of a good deal of symbolism.

Both these sects were popular among the Heian aristocrats and the imperial court. Their monks had free access to most aristocratic houses, where they were employed to pray for the success of their patron and the failure of his enemies. Buddhism became more and more a private religion, then, as the government of the country shifted from imperial to private domination.

This tendency is seen most clearly in the luxurious private temples which began to spring up in Kyoto during the Heian period. The first of these is the Hōjō-ji, which was founded by Fujiwara Tadahira in about 924. Although it is no longer in existence, it is known to have been a most impressive sight, and the position of abbot at this temple was a coveted one. The major images of the temple were of Amida and Fudō. Amida is the ruler of the Pure Land and would look out for his followers after their deaths; Fudō was considered a powerful symbol able to protect his followers from harm in this world.

There was yet another temple called Hōjō-ji, although the name is written in different Chinese characters, this one built by Fujiwara Michinaga, the most famous member of the Fujiwara clan, in 1018, at the height of his power. This temple, too, was constructed on an extravagant scale and service in it was important to the monks of the time.

Both of these temples had strong ties to Enryaku-ji, the major temple of the Tendai sect, a fact which demonstrates the importance of Tendai in the very best Heian social circles. Neither of them, nor any of the other private temples,[2] has any particular importance from a philosophical or religious standpoint, but they provided a highly visible link between the clergy and the aristocracy and demonstrate the important role Buddhism played in the daily lives of the aristocrats. They stood as symbols of the interdependence of the monks and the nobles; this interdependence is obviously important in any discussion of the audience of *Konjaku Monogatari-shū* which starts with the premise that the compiler was a monk.

To appreciate the nature of this interdependence and the important role religion played in the lives of the Heian aristocracy (especially during the *insei* period) one need only look through some of the diaries kept by Heian court nobles. In the year 1111, for example, the devout aristocrat could have spent at least 40 percent of the days of the year involved in some sort of Buddhist activity. Most of these were sutra readings, dedications of images, and various other ceremonies performed both at the court and at private homes. Fujiwara Munetada, whose diary *Chūyūki* is one of our major sources of information for the social history of the times, is a good case in point. Over one period of five years he averaged about eight or nine days out of every thirty-day month in some sort of religious activity. The ceremonies were often lavish events, lasting for long periods of time and featuring a good deal of preaching.[3]

The diaries contain a wealth of information concerning the external trappings of the ceremonies, giving detailed descriptions of the types of robes worn, the order in which the participants entered the room, the questions of precedence which inevitably arose and the like. We know that ceremonies often featured music and dancing, and they have even been compared with the *uta-awase,* or poetry contest;[4] externally, in any event, they were most definitely aristocratic events.

The diaries do not, however, speak of the actual content of the sermons even though they usually mention that preaching took place, the preacher was so-and-so, and sometimes say that the audience was "moved to tears" by the sermon. Even so, it is possible to speculate about the contents of the sermons on the basis of other evidence.

The most important source of information in this regard is a work called *Hyakuza Hōdan Kikigaki-shō,* a record of a hundred-day ceremony to dedicate a copy of the Lotus Sutra, held at the temple Daian-ji beginning on the eighteenth day of the second month of 1110. The test of this work is interspersed with stories of the type to be found in *Konjaku Monogatari-shū* and other *setsuwa* collections, and from its existence we can speculate that stories were a part of the preacher's fare. Preachers apparently used the stories to make certain Buddhist points, and one might assume that a powerful or moving story would have been important in catching and holding the attention of the audience.[5]

In addition to *Hyakuza Hōdan Kikigaki-shō* and another work somewhat similar to it, we also know that Buddhist monks were in the habit of visiting aristocrats at their homes and sometimes told them stories to illustrate certain points. At least two fairly well-developed tales are recorded in Munetada's diary.[6]

Being frequent listeners to stories told by Buddhist monks, the aristocrats were apparently rather critical in their tastes. Munetada, for all the time he spent at Buddhist ceremonies, seldom praised the speakers, though he occasionally notes that someone's preaching "caused tears to well up in the eyes of the audience," or the like. When the preacher has been particularly effective it is often mentioned that he has been rewarded, usually with a horse, robe or the like. These rewards were important to the monks, and doubtless they made it their business to understand just what the aristocrats would think beautiful so that they might be rewarded more frequently.

We can see how this worked by considering the case of a monk called Yōen (1047–1125). His name often appears as speaker in diaries from the period. We know that he enjoyed considerable popularity among the aristocrats, and was considered a good preacher. The reason for this popularity is made clear in *Uji Shūi Monogatari* 42, a story in which he is the hero.

In this tale, Yōen is given a poem as a present for having delivered a sermon, and subsequently refuses to present it to another person because he recognizes its value; the tale concludes with the statement, "How impressive to see such devotion to artistic pursuits!" It seems reasonable to assume that any successful preacher in this period would have had familiarity with these "artistic pursuits" and would have used this familiarity to impress his aristocratic listeners in the hopes of receiving generous rewards.

Such is the nature of the interdependent relationship between the aristocracy and the clergy. The aristocrats were aware that they were living in a degenerate age—there are many comments on this fact in their diaries—and they spent a good deal of time engaged in religious practices. The monks, for their part, found their connections to the nobility profitable both economically and socially.

Now it has been suggested by some scholars that *Konjaku Monogatari-shū* is a collection of tales intended primarily for an audience of the lower classes, for people who were illiterate and ignorant of court culture.[7] Although it is probably true that some of the audiences were of the lower classes, I cannot accept the theory for several reasons, mainly because the evidence shows that preaching was aimed first at the aristocratic classes, and that stories were commonly used in this preaching. There would have been very little profit in preaching to the commoners, and the monks certainly did not turn their backs on worldly considerations.

Tendai Buddhism, in particular, appealed to the aristocracy from a philosophical standpoint as well as an aesthetic one. This sect's thought has been characterized as "absolute monism," which means that "all things of the actual world come to be absolutely affirmed as identical with those of the enlightened world."[8] In other words, man is identified with the Buddha, defilement with enlightenment, the actual world with the eternal world, and so on.

This has two major implications which must be taken into account when considering the nature of *Konjaku*. The first is that by not denying the present world Tendai was an affirmative force which had meaning in the present; one could hope to achieve profit in the present world through an acceptance of Tendai. This harkens back to the idea that the proper role of Buddhism was to help preserve the power of the imperial family. The second is that such a view encourages the use of what is called *upāya* (*hōben* in Japanese), a doctrine which holds that any method used to bring a person to the truth—even a lie—is acceptable. One might tell falsehoods if the ultimate goal was to increase the wisdom of the listeners: if good and evil are seen as complementary rather than as exclusive, almost any story could contain a religious moral.

Thus Tendai affirmed the validity of the aristocrats' lives, and stressed the desirability of success in the present world. On the other hand, it included a belief in Amida, whose Pure Land is essentially a denial of the present world. So Tendai offered simultaneously one set of rituals to assist the believer in his present life and another one to help him obtain salvation in the next.

The spread of Pure Land belief in Japan is linked to the idea of *mappō*, or a belief the world had reached a point where the true teaching of the Buddha was so obscured by the passage of time and the emergence of false doctrine that it was now impossible to obtain enlightenment by one's own power. Amida's Pure Land was a land in which cares would fade away and the devout would be able to devote all their attention to their Buddhist practices; to obtain rebirth in this paradise was the eventual goal of Pure Land believers. Clearly a sincere belief in Pure Land tenets entails a denial of the validity of the present existence.

Now the earliest aristocratic perceptions of Pure Land belief simply ignored this denial of worldly values and concentrated on the glorious nature of the Pure Land. The rich and powerful interpreted their present life as already being the "Pure Land," and they celebrated their earthly glory. As the Heian period wore on, however, and aristocratic dominance began to give way to a period of chaos, noblemen began to redefine their image of the Pure Land. The *insei* period was, as we have seen, a time of instability, and as is common during such periods, religion flourished. The aristocrats put more and more of their energy into seeking salvation in the life to come.

One of the figures which seized the imagination of the aristocrats most strongly during the time *Konjaku* was being compiled was that of the *hijiri,* or holy man, a person who gained fame by his rejection of fame, who was seen as holding the ideals of established Buddhism in contempt and was revered for this. The *hijiri* are, collectively, among the most important figures described in the pages of *Konjaku*. They are almost inevitably associated with Pure Land belief in the rebirth in the Western Paradise, but they are also generally associated with the Lotus Sutra, a sutra which promises great benefits in this world for its devotees.

Such, then, is the complex background that nurtured the monk who compiled *Konjaku Monogatari-shū*. The state-oriented early Buddhism had gradually shifted to a Buddhism of the aristocracy, and was beginning to undergo yet another transformation, this time to a more popular phase. It would be a mistake, however, to say that it was antiaristocratic or overly popular, for the ties between the clergy and the aristocracy continued to be complex. It is now time to consider some of the various theories concerning the authorship of *Konjaku*. Although the traditional theory has been thoroughly discredited, I will begin with an examination of it, for an understanding of the traditional view of *Konjaku*.

The Traditional Theory

For many years the compiler of *Konjaku Monogatari-shū* was assumed to be Minamoto Takakuni (1004–1077), an aristocrat who rose to the rank of Major Councilor (Dainagon) of Uji. He is known to have been a lover of stories and was slightly eccentric as well. He thus seemed to many the natural candidate. To understand how the Takakuni theory developed we must turn our attention briefly to one of the most troublesome ghosts that continues to haunt *setsuwa* scholars, the now-defunct *Uji Dainagon Monogatari*.

In the preface of the present-day *Uji Shūi Monogatari* we are given the picture of an aging Takakuni on summer retreat at his palace in Uji (near the present city of Kyoto), in the following posture:

. . . with his topknot up, looking quite unusual, he spread out a cushion where he could be cool. He had someone fan him with a large fan, and summoned travelers from the road, caring not whether they were of high or low rank. These people he asked to recite stories. He himself lay sprawled out inside his screen, writing things down just as they were recited in a large notebook.[9]

Takakuni's collection, this preface goes on to tell us, contained stories from India, China, and Japan: "Among them are holy stories, unusual stories, frightening stories, moving stories, disgusting stories, even a few stories which are not true; there are stories of cleverness and various other kinds of stories." The collection which resulted from Takakuni's practice of hailing travelers from the road was added to by later enthusiasts, the preface states, growing larger as it circulated.

It was long assumed that the collection thus described was none other than the collection we now know as *Konjaku Monogatari-shū*. It is identified in the *Uji Shūi* preface as "Uji Dainagon Monogatari," and the assumption was that this was merely another of the several names for the present *Konjaku*. In 1668 Hayashi Michiharu, a bibliographical scholar, distinguished between "Uji Dainagon Monogatari" and "Konjaku Monogatari," saying that the former was indeed the work of Takakuni; in a later work, however, Hayashi's son treats these two titles as one, stating that *Konjaku* was the work of Takakuni. This appears to be the source of the confusion. [10]

Scholars are now fairly certain that there did exist a work known as "Uji Dainagon Monogatari" and that it was probably one of the sources for the *Konjaku* compiler. There is no particular reason to assume that this work was not the creation of Takakuni. Since Takakuni died in 1077 we can probably place the earliest possible date for the compilation of *Konjaku* at about 1070, for it is presumed that Takakuni finished his collection near the end of his life, and the *Konjaku* compiler would have needed some time to read it and to gather his own tales.

The best evidence against the Takakuni theory is the text of *Konjaku Monogatari-shū* itself. It is difficult to imagine that a work so massive, so well organized, and using so many written sources for its tales could have been compiled in such a haphazard manner as is described in the *Uji Shūi* preface. Since the preface is the only primary evidence for the theory, if "Uji Dainagon Monogatari" is acknowledged to be a separate work there is no reason at all to believe that Takakuni had anything to do with *Konjaku*.

The Takakuni theory died hard, however, and has not yet been completely laid to rest. Its major attraction has been that Takakuni was known as a storyteller and that it would therefore be reasonable to assume that a collection of well-told stories must have been produced by this skillful narrator. The existence and slow death of the Takakuni theory are of importance to us now because they demonstrate the qualities traditionally associated with *Konjaku:* skillful narration and no real purpose other than the love of a good story. [11]

The stories to be found in *Konjaku,* however, are more than examples of skillful narration; they are for the most part stories with a point. Nineteen of the collection's thirty-one volumes contain Buddhist tales, and as we shall see in a later chapter, the entire organization of the collection is Buddhist. Sutras, commentaries on sutras, and Chinese miracle tales about sutras, in addition to a host of Buddhist tale collections, have served as sources for many of the stories in *Konjaku*. Thus it is not surprising that most scholars now agree that the compiler was either a Buddhist monk or a layman with a deep concern with Buddhism. Let us now turn to an examination of two of the most recent and compelling theories concerning the identity of this monk.

The Monk: Tōdai-ji or Mt. Hiei?

Two major theories have been advanced about the identity of the postulated Buddhist monk compiler of *Konjaku Monogatari-shū* recently, and both are backed by persuasive arguments if not by definitive evidence. One holds that the compiler was a Tendai monk living on Mt. Hiei, the Tendai headquarters, and was associated with the Eshin faction of Tendai, founded by the monk Genshin (942–1017). The other is even more specific, claiming that the compiler was one Kakujū (1084–1140), a monk serving in the Tōdai-ji temple in Nara.

The Kakujū theory is one of the most recent to be published in Japan and has gained some popularity. In 1948 the great *Konjaku* scholar Katayose Masayoshi suggested that Kakujū might be an important figure in the compilation of *Konjaku,* but stopped short of saying he was the compiler.[12] Kakujū's connection with *Konjaku* was postulated on the basis of his supposed connection with a Chinese collection of tales in praise of the Lotus Sutra. This work, *Hung-tsan Fa-hua Ch'uan,* was probably imported into Japan in 1120, if not before, and it has ten tales which Katayose finds in *Konjaku*. Of these, five are direct borrowings and five he classifies as indirect borrowings. Katayose speculates that if *Hung-tsan Fa-hua Ch'uan* was, indeed, brought to Japan in 1120, then it is obvious that *Konjaku* could not have been compiled before that year. This is one of the main reasons for refuting the Takakuni theory of authorship since he died in 1077.

Kakujū was a monk who was well known for his skills as both a scholar and a preacher. He was an accomplished poet, and the son of a Minamoto high official, so his secular standing was impeccable. He is known to have been popular as a preacher in aristocratic ceremonies. His office was a repository for imported

secret documents from China, so he must have been familiar with
most of the Chinese Buddhist works available in Japan. Thus
Katayose speculates that Kakujū was probably the link between
the *Konjaku* compiler and the Chinese work in question.

Recently Sakai Kenji has taken this argument one step further,
eliminating the middle man, and has speculated that Kakujū was
more than a link to the *Konjaku* compiler. His conclusions come
as the result of certain editorial marks he has discovered in the
text that is considered the oldest extant *Konjaku* manuscript, the
so-called Suzuka MS. [13]

Sakai's arguments are technical and difficult to summarize, but
they have seized the imaginations of many Japanese scholars and
some understanding of them is important to the student of *Konjaku*.
They are the first arguments based on new evidence that
the debate over the identity of the compiler has seen in some
years.

The editorial marks in question were first noticed by a nine-
teenth-century bibliographer, Ban Nobutomo (1773–1846). In
1839 Nobutomo reported seeing a volume VII of *Konjaku* in a
manuscript he estimated to be six or seven hundred years old.
He later saw that volume and two others from the same manuscript and was able, from a notation on it, to identify it as having
been made at a building in the Nara temple complex Tōdai-ji.

Sakai subjected this manuscript to a thorough search and has
turned up a total of five such manuscript notations in four different volumes. He is apparently the first modern scholar to notice
the remarks of Nobutomo and follow them up. Sakai concludes
that the notations were made at the Tōdai-ji; from this it is only
a short step to the speculation that the original *Konjaku* was also
prepared at that temple. He maintains that the person most likely
to have been the compiler was Kakujū.

It remains impossible to date the MS in question precisely,
and at least one scholar holds that Sakai is totally wrong in his
assessment of its age. This is Hirabayashi Shigetoku, who concludes from a search through temple records that the building
identified with Tōdai-ji—called the Shinsōin—was probably not
erected until 1444. Thus, Hirabayashi asserts, if the building

referred to is the Shinsōin of Tōdai-ji, Kakujū would have been long since dead and could have had nothing to do with either the manuscript or the compilation of *Konjaku;* if it is a different Shinsōin, Kakujū is ruled out for different reasons.[14]

In the absence of any definitive proof Sakai's arguments must be considered speculative, no matter how appealing they may seem. They cannot be ruled out, but it is difficult to accept them uncritically.

The theory that the compiler of *Konjaku* was a Tendai monk living at Mt. Hiei is older than the Kakujū theory, but every bit as speculative. This theory has been presented persuasively recently by Takahashi Mitsugu, whose arguments depend on the interpretation of internal evidence rather than on the dating of manuscripts. Takahashi finds many stories in *Konjaku* which he postulates were transmitted by Mt. Hiei monks and were probably not commonly told anywhere else. From this and certain other evidence he concludes that the compiler must have been a Mt. Hiei monk.[15]

Some of this other evidence is worth surveying briefly. Takahashi has found, for example, ninety names of monks who had direct or indirect ties to Tendai in the scrolls of *Konjaku,* and only thirty names of monks with ties to Shingon, the other major Heian sect. Further, he finds tales about the monk Ryōgen of the sort that would have only been told by his supporters. Ryōgen (912–985), who was Genshin's teacher, was a controversial figure involved in a good deal of intertemple warfare, especially that carried out between Enryaku-ji, the main temple on Mt. Hiei, and Miidera, the second most powerful Tendai temple, which was not located on Mt. Hiei. Stories about Ryōgen, according to Takahashi, carry an Enryaku-ji slant.

In addition, many of the stories in volume VI, Takahashi notes, prominently mention the vow of Yakushi, the healing Buddha, and frequently the compiler has altered the story as it appeared in its Chinese source in order to stress this vow. The central devotional hall at Mt. Hiei venerated Yakushi.

Takahashi's conclusions are largely a matter of how one decides to interpret the internal textual evidence in *Konjaku,* but they do have the force of numbers. There is no particular reason, for example, to believe that the compiler went out of his way to stress the Yakushi vow in his volume VI tales merely because this was the image worshiped at a temple to which he himself belonged, but if we put this fact together with others pointing to a Tendai compiler it assumes more significance.

In any event, there is no denying the fact that the compiler is very much in sympathy with Genshin and his school. Genshin had his headquarters at Mt. Hiei and was a disciple of Ryōgen, a controversial figure whom the *Konjaku* compiler respected. This is at least suggestive of Tendai/Mt. Hiei involvement or orientation. The evidence is circumstantial, but persuasive nonetheless.

Summary

In the absence of definitive evidence concerning the identity of the compiler of *Konjaku Monogatari-shū* we have little choice but to step back and listen to what the text itself has to tell us. Unfortunately, texts have a way of saying different things to different people, and it is doubtful that the debate will ever really end. There are some points, however, that I believe can be made and defended by a reading of the stories in *Konjaku;* if these will not tell us who the compiler was, at least they will tell us something about him.

The compiler of *Konjaku* was aware that he was living in bad times, and his collection can be seen as a personal reaction to his situation. He offers his audience a plan for success in this world that is largely dependent on Buddhist thought, as we shall see in Chapter 3. That, plus the fact that he was widely read in a vast number of Buddhist works, tells us that he himself was a Buddhist monk. Most likely he had had considerable experience as a preacher, for although he shows concern with the entertainment of his audience he is even more interested in getting a message across.

The evidence suggests that the type of audience at which this preaching was aimed was aristocratic. This is not only because we know that most preaching during the Heian period was directed at this class, but because, as we shall see, the compiler makes use of certain editorial techniques which can be linked with aristocratic aesthetic principles.

The compiler's favorable treatment of Genshin and the idea of rebirth in the Western Paradise of Amida, plus his obvious respect for the Lotus Sutra, leads me to believe that he was indeed a Tendai monk; I would go so far as to speculate that he was an adherent to the Eshin school on Mt. Hiei, though I would stress that this is only speculation. I will present a more detailed picture of his religious vision in Chapter 3. Before doing that, however, I shall proceed to a consideration of the genre to which *Konjaku Monogatari-shū* belongs, and its position within that genre.

Chapter Two

Konjaku Monogatari-shū in the *Setsuwa* Tradition

Konjaku Monogatari-shū stands at the fountainhead of a literary genre known as *setsuwa bungaku,* or *setsuwa* literature. This genre is composed of collections of tales, the overwhelming majority of which are Buddhist. The collections are an integral part of the Buddhist tradition of the Heian and Kamakura periods, but one should not assume that they sprang up out of nowhere to be used by Buddhist preachers. They have, on the contrary, demonstrable ties to Japanese myth and other forms of oral literature, and are best understood in the overall context of Japanese literature.

In this chapter *Konjaku* will be examined in the light of its genre so that we can come to a better understanding of what makes it unique. It will be necessary to discuss *setsuwa* in general before attempting to locate *Konjaku* among the many such collections produced in the Heian and Kamakura periods.

Setsuwa, Oral Tradition, and Myth

The word *setsuwa* is a modern term, and the student who combs through contemporary documents for references to them during the Heian or Kamakura periods will find little to indicate that the collections even existed. The reason for this is that they were considered as something other than literature by the aristocratic readers of the time. This does not mean that these aristocrats disliked or looked down on stories or the collection of stories, however; even a poet of the stature of Kamo no Chōmei (1153–1216), author of the well-known *Hōjōki* [An Account of My Hut], made a *setsuwa* collection. We have already seen that

Minamato Takakuni, an aristocrat, was famous for his love of stories and was thought by some to be the compiler of *Konjaku Monogatari-shū*. Still other aristocrats transmitted stories in their diaries, and many of the *setsuwa* extant today clearly had their beginnings in court gossip.

The stories were collected for reasons other than literary. Usually this had something to do with Buddhism, but this is not to say that a story given a Buddhist interpretation by any given compiler of a *setsuwa* collection necessarily had a Buddhist origin. Indeed, it is often the case that zealous Buddhist preachers have appropriated stories told originally in a totally different context and given these stories a new, Buddhist interpretation in the telling of them.

The important thing to remember is that *setsuwa* were seldom told for their own sake: they nearly always were transmitted for a reason. This reason would then work to reshape the tale, and we must recognize that different versions of the same tale should not be thought of as variants from a fixed source, but rather as independent stories.

Although the stories were told at least in part for their educational value, they were obviously entertaining in the first place. Their subject matter was usually out of the ordinary.

As narratives, *setsuwa* have three major characteristics which should be borne in mind:

1. They are generally short, taking no more than five or six written pages.

2. They are centered around some event, and the emphasis is on this event rather than the hero. Titles are thus often of the "How So-and-so encountered such-and-such and did such-and-such" variety.

3. The event depicted is almost always extraordinary in nature, but it is not something which would have been considered implausible by a contemporary audience.

In short, *setsuwa* have a "ring of truth" to them; they are closer to histories than to fabrications. One calls to mind the fact that early novels in English often had titles such as *The History of Tom*

Jones, and that early novelists went to great lengths to make their stories appear true to readers.

That *setsuwa* were born in oral tradition and nurtured by oral transmission as well as by written transmission should be obvious. A more difficult question is that of deciding to what extent they should be classified as written literature and to what extent they are oral, for it is true that they have a foot in both camps, so to speak. The life history of a typical *setsuwa* might look something like this: something happens which is out of the ordinary, and stories begin to circulate about it; the stories are transmitted orally for a time by those who are interested in them; a version is recorded in a *setsuwa* collection; the story continues to circulate, told both by people who have heard it and people who have read it. It might work its way into subsequent collections, passed on by compilers who are familiar with it either from word of mouth or in its written version.

Clearly a story which circulated in this way would have no fixed form, but would be told by people who had some reason for stressing one or another aspect of it. It is impossible to overstate the importance of content and the lack of importance of form in tales such as these; because they were transmitted for content their forms changed readily, conforming to the individual perceptions of the stories' content as held by different narrators.

There are numerous examples of this, but I will limit myself to one found in the diary of a late Heian aristocrat which seems to show the type of life experienced by most *setsuwa*. The story in question is found in *Chūyūki,* the diary of Fujiwara Munetada.

On the twelfth day of the second month in 1120 Munetada reports that he has been visited by the monk Keizen of the temple Miidera. The two talked and Keizen told Munetada two stories which he recorded in his diary; there were possibly others told as well. One of these concerns a monk from Miidera who broke his vows and moved to the capital with his wife and family. He kept pheasants and came to be known by the scornful name "Pheasant Monk." When he was stricken with a serious illness and was told the end was near, however, he experienced a surge of faith and renewed his religious vows, selling his property to commission a picture of Amida. Eventually he was told in a dream that he would be reborn in the Western Paradise, and Keizen appeared certain that this had indeed happened.

This particular tale was told by a monk from Miidera and concerns a miracle connected with that temple; it is not difficult to imagine that Keizen was attempting to elicit financial or political support for his temple. Keizen also seems to have used the story as a part of a modest sermon, for Munetada tells us that the monk added a moral:

Keizen said that when we consider this it will show us the validity of Amida's vow not to abandon even the worst sinners, and accordingly those who wish to be reborn in the Western Paradise should devote themselves wholeheartedly to reciting the name of Amida.[1]

Munetada, on the other hand, had his own reason for writing the story down in his diary:

I have recorded these events because they are unusual. Truly although it is the latter period of the law, the time of the Buddha has not yet passed away.

So Munetada and Keizen have transmitted this tale for different reasons, and it is probable that their two versions of the story varied somewhat.

Keizen related the tale to the aristocrat Munetada, whom he doubtless knew to be interested in stories about rebirth in Amida's Western Paradise; had he been telling the story to a group of young monks as part of their education he would have stressed different parts of it. Had one of the people who lived near the "Pheasant Monk" been telling the story to a friend he would have stressed entirely different aspects. The story could conceivably be brought up in a discussion of rebirth in the Western Paradise of Amida, of monks who break their vows, or of people learning of their rebirth through a dream, among other possible contexts. It is easy enough to imagine that the purpose for which one would tell the story might differ so greatly that the versions related by different people would have very little in common.

As a story which stresses content over form the *setsuwa* is very like a genre folklorists know as belief legends.[2] These are stories which spring from some belief held by the teller and which are told in order to illustrate that belief. The particular details of the belief legend are not so important as the overall plausibility of the tale, and hence can easily vary from telling to telling. Probably the most flourishing example of this kind of story in the United States today is the UFO tale, or the story about unidentified flying objects and the visitors from outer space they presumably carry.

This is not to say, of course, that all *setsuwa* should be thought of as "belief legends," for clearly there is a range of tales included under the rubric *setsuwa*. It is true, however, that *setsuwa* tend to be about extraordinary events or to have been taken from the lives of well-known people, and are often told with an air that suggests, "Such incredible things *can* happen!" In *Konjaku* XXIX.40, for example, a monk falls asleep in a deserted place and awakens to find that a snake has taken his penis in its mouth and died from the experience; in this tale the compiler cautions us against napping in deserted places, as if to say that anything is possible.

Let us then move to a consideration of the nature of the events depicted in *setsuwa*. Many of them are clearly connected with Buddhism from beginning to end; this is especially true of stories such as that of the "Pheasant Monk" discussed above, or of the tales found in volume XV of *Konjaku Monogatari-shū*, all of which are about people reborn in the Western Paradise of Amida. Another category of tales is biography, for many *setsuwa* are taken from the lives of well-known people.

There is yet another category of stories, however, that is much older and more directly connected with Japanese myth or folktale, and this probably constitutes the original *setsuwa* told in Japan. Although these tales may have been given Buddhist interpretations by the compilers of various collections it is likely that they go much further back and represent versions of stories that were told before Buddhism ever entered the country.

It has been noted that *setsuwa* collections seldom if ever contain myth.[3] While this is true on one level, it is also true that there are certain similarities between *setsuwa* and myth that are suggestive and should be examined.

First let us clarify some of the differences between the two genres. Myths were told for entirely different reasons than were *setsuwa,* and were set in a different time period. Myths generally deal with origins and the exploits of deities, while *setsuwa* are set in the relatively recent past, clearly in human time, and generally serve as examples of extraordinary events. Japanese myths further tend to be centered around heroes and *setsuwa,* as we have seen, are centered around events.

What happened in Japan is a sort of secularization of myth. Stories were told and retold, and were gradually changed and redefined. I will clarify this by tracing two myths from their most mythlike stage to the form in which we find them in *Konjaku,* but first it will be necessary to introduce a collection which is an intermediate stage in the process, *Nihon Ryōiki.*

The full name of the first extant collection of *setsuwa* is *Nihonkoku Genpō Zen'aku Ryōiki* [A Record of Miraculous Events in Japan Connected with the Immediate Retribution for Good and Punishment for Evil]. It was compiled in the early ninth century by the monk Kyōkai, a *shamon,* or lay monk, who was connected with the temple Yakushi-ji in Nara. Kyōkai's motives for making this collection are spelled out in the preface to the first of its three volumes:

If not by pointing out the workings of the laws of cause and effect, how then could one hope to reform evil and advance good? . . . Why should only those happenings in other countries be respected and those of our own land not be held in awe?[4]

Kyōkai presents us with tales calculated to demonstrate in the most graphic manner possible the retribution for actions in this present life. The collection has been recognized as being the source of some eighty-one of the tales found in *Konjaku Monogatari-shū;* twenty-seven of these are found in the didactic volume XX, which contains many stories about retribution.

The language of *Ryōiki* is Chinese, but this is a particularly Japanese style of Chinese known as *hentai kambun* ("altered Chinese"), and would probably have been intelligible to the common people if they heard it read aloud. There is no question that the stories are subordinate to the didactic messages they contain. At the close of nearly every story, Kyōkai adds his own interpretation of the event he has just described. Frequently he quotes from a sutra or a commentary on a sutra to make his point, though sometimes he merely adds a personal comment, as at the end of II.28, a tale about how a poverty-stricken woman received money from a statue of Buddha: "We know, then, truly—this was because of the extraordinary power of the statue of Buddha and the rare faith of the woman."

It is thought by some scholars that many of the stories in *Ryōiki* were originated and disseminated by groups of *shamon*, those lay monks who went from place to place in Japan preaching to the common people and among whose ranks the compiler of *Ryōiki*, Kyōkai, is numbered.[5] Certain other stories, however, were probably well known at the time of Kyōkai and merely adapted by him. The collection itself, after its compilation, became a good source for later compilers, so Kyōkai's position in the history of *setsuwa* literature is obviously important.

The *shamon* were frequently from important families and they must have presented an impressive image to the world. We get a glimpse of such a person in *Ryōiki* III.14, which tells how a government official attempted to detain a *shamon* and was punished for it. In this story the *shamon* is a descendant of the Ono family, which traces its lineage back to the imperial family. When the *shamon* is struck by the official he tells the official that the power of the sutras he is carrying is awesome and that the official will soon see this for himself. True to the *shamon*'s promise, the official is catapulted through the air to the spot where he struck the *shamon;* he hangs suspended there for a full day before falling to his death.

When we consider the fact that many of the myths found in works like *Kojiki* and *Nihon Shoki,* two of the earliest recorded histories extant in Japan, had their origins in stories told to extoll the deities instrumental in the founding of certain powerful families, we can see how important the *shamon* were in the secularization of Japanese myth.

In ancient Japan the clans were virtually autonomous and their founding myths were probably told throughout the geographical areas they occupied. With the far-reaching reformation in 645 known as the Taika Reform, however, the nature of this clan system began to change. The central government and the imperial family came to have more and more authority, with the clans operating within the system rather than autonomously. These changes were taking place at about the same time Buddhism was being introduced and spread throughout Japan.

What appears to have happened, then, is that family founding myths and other stories associated with pre-Buddhist Japan continued to be told, but were gradually adapted by the Buddhists. Simply speaking, the values of one system eventually were supplanted by those of another system, and the stories which had been associated with the old religion were also taken over by the new. This process is apparent in several, though by no means all, of the tales found in *Nihon Ryōiki*.[6]

To illustrate this let us consider the case of a very popular tale in Japan, that of a mortal who is able to gain dominance over thunder. The first recording of this story is in *Nihon Shoki*, where it is recounted as an event which took place during the seventh year of Yūryaku (A.D.463). In the *Nihon Shoki* account the emperor commands a court official named Chiisakobe no Sugaru to go out and capture the thunder deity.[7] The official complies, and brings a large serpent back to the palace. The emperor is frightened because he has not purified himself, and orders the release of the deity. The deity, which has flaming eyeballs, is released in the hills and given a new name.

This story is used by Kyōkai in *Nihon Ryōiki* as the first story in his first volume. He makes some changes, however, which are worth examining. In the *Ryōiki* version the hero Sugaru inadvertently enters the emperor's chambers while the sovereign is making love to the empress. The emperor is embarrassed and stops his lovemaking; at that point the thunder rolls in the sky.

The emperor commands the official Sugaru to invite the thunder deity to his chambers, which the official does.

In response to the invitation the lightning strikes near Sugaru, who has it placed on a portable shrine and carried to the emperor. There is no reference in this tale to the form assumed by the deity. Once again the emperor is afraid, and this time, too, he has the thunder released after worshiping it. When Sugaru dies, however, the emperor has an inscription made for his tomb which reads, "The Tomb of Sugaru, Who Caught the Thunder." This angers the deity, which strikes the pillar bearing the inscription, but is caught fast there. Once again the deity is released and this time the inscription is changed to read, "The Tomb of Sugaru, Who Caught Thunder both during His Life and after His Death."[8]

As it is related in *Nihon Shoki* the story shows a deity which is clearly superior to the emperor. This fact marks the tale as being from a time before the dominance of the imperial family. It was probably told by the Chiisako clan and was used by them to explain their origins. Sugaru is a hero and is said to be a particularly strong man.

The attitude toward the deity undergoes a transformation in the *Ryōiki* tale, however. Here the emperor is also weak, and in the first part of the story the mortals are awed by the power of the thunder deity, but in the second part of the story—which is not present in the *Nihon Shoki* version—the thunder deity is shown to be something of a bumbler, unable to take revenge on the mortal who has defeated him. In this episode the emperor is more powerful than the deity, and we must conclude that the story dates from a time when the dominance of the state over the individual families was all but completed.

Kyōkai makes even more changes in this story within his collection. The third story in the first volume of *Ryōiki* is yet another treatment of the same general theme and is more secular because it moves completely away from an awed view of the native deities and introduces Buddhism to the drama.

In this story we have the introduction of a thunder deity who communicates more directly with mortals and is much less frightening to them. A farmer raises a metal rod during a shower and is surprised when the thunder deity appears before him in the form of a small child. (Chiisako, the family name of the hero discussed above, means "small child," and this provides one link between the two tales.) The farmer is about to strike the deity when the latter promises to send the farmer a child of his own if he will show mercy. Subsequently a child is born to the farmer. It is born with a snake coiled around its head, and grows to be a very strong man.

This child bests a famous strong man in a contest, then becomes an acolyte at the temple Gangō-ji, where he defeats an ogre who had been killing monks from the temple as they attempted to ring the temple bell. Later this hero becomes a lay brother and defeats a group of noblemen who will not allow the temple to irrigate its fields. Following this the hero is ordained and given the name Dōjō. There are many stories about his great strength, and elements of this particular tale appear in a variety of written sources.

The major elements in this story—an old man, an unusual birth, a child who shows supernatural affiliations, and some power to control the fall of rain—are common in many Japanese folktales. The deity here is more powerful than the ordinary mortal, but is still subject to control by the mortal. The metal rod has obviously given the farmer some special power. The thunder deity is associated with the dragon deity and has power over rain, the most important element in early Japanese folk religion. In the Sugaru tale the hero's success resulted in the founding of a new family; here, too, the emphasis is on a child and the special powers he has because of his unusual origin. Readers of Japanese folktales will readily recall a large number of stories with similar plot lines.

In the Dōjō story we have the introduction of the power of Buddhism over the native Shinto deities. Here we have a clear example of a relatively old story being appropriated by a Buddhist preacher who changes it to make it conform to his own purposes. This is but one demonstration of the pivotal role played by *Nihon*

Ryōiki in the transformation of native Japanese myths to a more Buddhistic form, the *setsuwa*.

To underscore the deep roots this Dōjō tale has in Japanese folk tradition it is necessary only to point to some of the similarities the story has to one of the most popular of the Japanese märchen, the story of Issun Bōshi, or "Little One Inch." The hero of Issun Bōshi is small—it will be recalled that the hero Sugaru had the family name "Chiisako," or "small child"—and he grows with the aid of a magic wand (in some instances it is a hammer), reminiscent of the metal rod the farmer uses to gain power over the thunder deity. The hero of Issun Bōshi defeats demons much as Dōjō does. Both characters are, moreover, usually associated with the water deity.[9]

Apparently the name *Dōjō* originally meant a primitive, private temple which was not yet completed.[10] This takes on more significance when we recall that the Dōjō tale in *Ryōiki* recounts the founding of the temple Gangō-ji. Dōjō is associated in Japanese oral tradition with the business of construction, having been identified as the builder of many bridges, buildings, and the like. In many versions of the Issun Bōshi tale, incidentally, the hero grows to normal size after waving a hammer; one is led to speculate that these tales may have been told by a family whose business was construction or smithing.

In any event, it seems perfectly reasonable to propose an allegorical reading of the *Ryōiki* story about Dōjō: the story dramatizes Shinto and Buddhist conflict, and eventual cooperation in the construction of a new Buddhist temple. Dōjō's actions are crucial because he is a mediator between the two forces, being a Buddhist lay brother on the one hand and the son of a Shinto deity on the other. His first adversary, the ogre who kills the monks of the temple when they attempt to ring the temple's bell, would be a local Shinto deity who resents having his territory invaded by Buddhists; Shinto deities appear to have been particularly offended by temple bells.[11] The second adversary—the noblemen who refuse to allow the temple to irrigate its fields—would be the families who were opposed to the importation of Buddhism to Japan.

Lest this seem too fanciful an interpretation of the story, let us turn our attention briefly to *Konjaku Monogatari-shū* XII.1, which also deals with conflict between Shinto and Buddhist forces, and includes the capture of the thunder deity by a mortal. The hero in this tale is a man known as Jinyō, who is described as a devout believer in the Lotus Sutra. The hero is called when thunder twice destroys a pagoda that a believer is attempting to build near a mountain temple. Jinyō works a spell with the Lotus Sutra and a young boy appears before him, begging for his freedom. When Jinyō asks why the deity is bent on destroying the pagoda, he replies:

The resident deity of this mountain is a close friend of mine. This resident deity said to me, "They are trying to build a pagoda over me. I will have no place to live; you come and destroy this pagoda." Because of this request I have twice destroyed the pagoda. But this time you have captured me with the power of the Lotus Sutra. So I will quickly move the deity to another place and give up this sinning.

The monk then makes the deity pledge to irrigate the temple's rice fields before he will release his hold. This the deity does immediately. Thereafter there is no problem with the pagoda, and the *Konjaku* compiler informs us that this miracle has taken place because of both the power of the Lotus Sutra and the sincerity of Jinyō and the man who has vowed to build the pagoda.

In this story the conflict which was lurking beneath the surface of the Dōjō/Gangō-ji tale has been brought out in the open. There is a direct conflict between the Shinto deity and the interests of Buddhism, and the Buddhists are the undisputed winners. This is not a merging of two belief systems, for there is no cooperation between them; the Buddhists have the upper hand and are able to give the orders. The hero gains control over the deity not by means of a Shinto charm such as the metal rod the farmer used in the Dōjō tale, but with a Buddhist weapon, the Lotus Sutra.

The gradual transformation of this story is a highly complex process and I have only begun to scratch the surface of it in my treatment here. Essentially the tale represents the move from

native Japanese myth—which grew, in this case, from the clan
system of ancient Japan—to an overtly Buddhist didactic story.
In all versions there are certain elements which do not change.
There is always a small child involved, some kind of human
dominance over the deity, and some agricultural significance—
domination over the deity means that the mortals can control the
fall of rain. This was an important skill for the rice farmer, who
depended on large amounts of rain at specific times.

Let us turn to another story to add more details to the map
of the route from myth to *setsuwa*. The story I have in mind has
to do with a mortal woman having intercourse with a deity. In
such tales, the deity generally takes the form of a snake. It might
be noted parenthetically that this motif is common in all parts
of the world—the English dragon (who actually resembles a large
worm more than a snake), for example, is said to be "avid for
maidens,"[12] and there is at least one instance of Apollo transforming himself into a snake in order to take advantage of a
young woman.[13]

There is a story in *Kojiki* that deals with this motif; it is
recorded as something that happened during the reign of Emperor
Sujin (97–30 B.C.). In this tale we are told that a woman who
was very beautiful was courted by a man of unparalleled appearance and dignity who would come to visit her every night at
midnight. In due course the woman became pregnant, and when
she was questioned by her father she told him of her secret lover.
At the suggestion of her parents the young woman scattered red
clay by the bed and threaded hemp yarn to a needle, sewing this
to the hem of her lover's garment. The next morning the family
followed the yarn trail through the keyhole of the door to Mt.
Miwa, where it ended at the shrine of the mountain deity.

The purpose of this story was to show that the child born from
this union —the founder of the Miwa clan—was a deity.[14] We
never see the deity in any other than his human form, but the
fact that he left the house through the keyhole indicates that he
took the form of a snake. It is likely that the tale is related to
some ritual involving the marriage of a mortal woman to a deity;
the woman in question was probably a shaman *(miko)*, and the

marriage to the deity would have been a part of her initiation ceremony. The story is a very old one, in any event, and there is no shame attached to the woman's having had sexual intercourse with a snake because the snake is a deity.

In most tales concerning intercourse between mortal women and snakes, however, the act is regarded as repulsive and to be avoided at all costs. Consider, for example, *Ryōiki* II.41, which tells how a woman is picking mulberry leaves when a snake crawls out onto the branch she is on. She is frightened and falls to the ground. The snake also falls to the ground, and it crawls into her vagina while she is unconscious. Her parents send for a doctor, who prepares a brew of ashes from burned millet stalks, hot water, and boar's hair. When five gallons of this have been poured into her vaginal opening the snake appears and dies, and when nine gallons have been poured in, all of the eggs are flushed out. The woman revives, her health regained.

Three years later, though, she dies, having once again been violated by a snake. Kyōkai, the *Ryōiki* compiler, draws two morals from this tale. The first is that medicine is indeed a wonderful art and one which is very important; the second is that the woman must have committed some sin in a former life to have become so attractive to snakes. He gives appropriate examples from the sutras to prove this second point.

There is on the surface virtually no similarity between this story and the *Kojiki* tale I discussed above, and one might be tempted to say that the two come from entirely different traditions. The fact that in the *Ryōiki* tale the woman is engaged in the making of silk, however, indicates that the story originally had religious significance, for sericulture was considered an especially holy act and was often the province of the shaman. The mulberry tree itself is holy—in one version of the Dōjō story, for example, the farmer is standing by a mulberry tree when he gains control over the thunder deity. Thus it is likely that the *Ryōiki* story is a considerably changed version of a tale similar to the *Kojiki* version—both depict the marriage of a mortal woman and a deity who has taken the form of a snake.

Salvation for the woman—temporary though it may have been—in the *Ryōiki* tale comes from a secular doctor and not, as one might expect, from a Buddhist monk. The same story is recorded with only minor changes in *Konjaku Monogatari-shū* XXIV.9, and salvation here also comes from a doctor. In oral versions alive today, however, Buddhism is introduced into the story and the woman is in some versions saved from conception through her participation in Buddhist activities. Generally, however, she is saved in other ways.

In its contemporary oral form, incidentally, the tale is a part of what is called the *oda maki* ("spool of thread") cycle, and is thought by Japanese scholars to be related to an old Shinto belief that deities paid yearly visits to mortals.[15] In all cases conception is seen as undesirable.

There are other tales in *Konjaku* about snakes that violate women, and in each case the act is seen as repulsive and to be avoided. For example, a woman in XXIX.39 squats to urinate by a bush and is violated by a snake. Although these tales seem at first glance to be rather bizarre affairs it is clear that they have their origins in ancient religious practices. They call to mind the Western tales involving a maiden, a dragon, and a valiant hero; their existence urges more research of a comparative nature.[16]

The two examples discussed above can be seen as stories which have been gradually transformed from myth to more Buddhist-oriented *setsuwa*. It should not be thought that this type of transformation process is the only way that *setsuwa* are related to the broader oral tradition in Japan, however; I think it is likely that elements of completely unrelated tales have on occasion been attached to Buddhist stories to create a hybrid sort of story that would have had a wide appeal because of its familiarity.

An example of this might be *Konjaku* XI.24, the story of Kume no Sennin and the founding of the temple Kume-dera. In this story the hero, who has attained supernatural powers, is flying over a stream when he notices a woman washing her clothes; he is overcome with desire for her and lands, marrying the woman and losing his supernatural powers. When the residents of his village are given a nearly impossible task to perform, Kume regains his supernatural abilities and does the work, for which he is granted a tract of land where he has a temple built.

This tale would appear to be a simple story explaining the founding of a temple, and hence a completely Buddhist story, but there are some noteworthy similarities between it and a popular folktale that merit consideration. The folktale in question is called the "Heavenly Wife" story; it describes how a farmer who has gone to a stream to bathe discovers a feathered robe belonging to a celestial female bather. He takes the robe and renders the woman powerless to return to the heavens, insisting that she remain on earth as his wife. This she does, and the couple has children, but the wife yearns to return to her home in the sky. When she discovers the hiding place of the robe she returns, after leaving instructions to her husband on how to join her.

He eventually does join her in heaven, but her father proves opposed to their marriage and assigns a series of impossible tasks to the husband. He performs them all successfully with supernatural help from his wife, but the couple is eventually parted forever, becoming stars on opposite sides of the Milky Way.[17]

I am not suggesting that the story about Kume was derived from this folktale, or that there is any of the transformation described above to be found here. It is worth noting, however, that the two tales have several key points in common. Both the heavenly woman and Kume lose their powers in action associated with water and bathing, although the circumstances are quite different in the two tales. In the folktale we might assume the man is being rewarded for making a proper religious purification; in the Kume tale the opposite would appear to be true, with Kume losing his powers because of the pollution of a body of water by the washing of clothes in it.[18]

Both the woman and Kume eventually regain their powers, however, and use them to aid mortals who have been assigned impossible tasks. After this noble act, both characters once again lose their powers, this time forever. We have already seen the importance of water deities in Japanese religion and oral tradition, so it should not be surprising to see that the source of power for both the woman and Kume appears to be somehow connected with water.

What we have here are two separate stories that make use of remarkably similar motifs. It is certainly suggestive that the Kume tale, used here in the history section of the Japanese Buddhist tales in *Konjaku Monogatari-shū*, should be so similar to a folktale which has nothing to do with Buddhism. We are left to conclude that the ties between some of the *setsuwa* in works like *Konjaku* and Japanese oral tradition are significant and that the *Konjaku* compiler was working actively within the Japanese oral tradition, using popular motifs in the construction of his stories.[19]

In summary, it is safe to say that there is a viable connection between ancient belief and myth on the one hand and *setsuwa* on the other. It is likely that some *setsuwa* had their roots in Japanese myth and that works such as *Nihon Ryōiki*, and traveling monks, had a great deal to do with the eventual transformation of these myths. In addition to these stories, it is reasonable to assume that others of the tales found in the *setsuwa* collections owe a considerable debt to Japanese oral tradition and folktales in general. Still others are oral because they began with some historical event and were told by word of mouth before being written down.

Precisely how many *setsuwa* can be traced back to ancient stories remains to be discovered, but the basic connection cannot be denied. We will now move to a consideration of the various types of *setsuwa* collections produced in the Heian and Kamakura periods.

Setsuwa Collections: A Classification

From the compilation of *Nihon Ryōiki* around 821 to the end of the Kamakura period in 1333 it is likely that more than one hundred collections of *setsuwa* were put together and about forty-five collections or fragments of collections are still extant. *Konjaku Monogatari-shū* is the largest and most comprehensive of these collections, and it shares stories with a good number of them. In his translation of *Uji Shūi Monogatari* D. E. Mills has provided information on nearly all of the extant collections up to 1333,[20] and I shall therefore confine my discussion to a few of the major works with close ties to *Konjaku*. By doing so I hope to define *Konjaku*'s position in the genre as a whole.

In order to identify *Konjaku*'s major characteristics more conveniently I propose a classification of *setsuwa* collections into three major types:

1. Collections intended primarily for use by Buddhist preachers for the instruction of the audience.

2. Collections which were intended primarily for the entertainment of their audience.

3. Collections which were intended primarily for the salvation of the compiler.

In order to show why I think *Konjaku Monogatari-shū* should be placed in the first of these categories I will discuss some of the more important collections from each category and compare them to *Konjaku*.

Collections Used by Buddhist Preachers.   I have already discussed *Nihon Ryōiki*, the first extant *setsuwa* collection, and would only note here that it would be the first collection placed in this category. The second extant collection of tales, *Sambō E Kotoba*, could also be placed in this category. I will discuss *Sambō E Kotoba, Dai-Nihon Hokke Genki, Hyakuza Hōdan Kikigaki-shō*, and *Uchigiki-shū* as representatives of this group. The fact that all of these works are relatively early mirrors the fact that the original impetus for the collection of *setsuwa* came from the needs of Buddhist preachers.

Sambō E Kotoba, a collection of sixty-two stories, is one of the relatively few for which both author and purpose can be identified. The compiler was Minamoto Tamenori, who made the collection around 984 to explain Buddhism to a young aristocratic lady who had recently taken the vows and become a nun. The work is divided into three volumes, one for each of the "Three Treasures" of Buddhism (the *Sambō* of the title); it was apparently illustrated as well (*E* means "picture," and *kotoba* is "word"). Although it may not have been used strictly for preaching it was clearly intended as an educational collection and aimed at the salvation of its readers.

Tamenori held a brief against the writers of the romances so popular in the Heian court:

Now, those things which we call romances are things which turn the heads of women. . . . They give names to fish, insects and the like as though such creatures were human; cause creatures which cannot speak to speak, and attribute feelings to that which has no feeling.[21]

Sambō E Kotoba offers chiefly a history of Buddhism in Japan and a series of stories about the major Buddhist celebrations of Japan. It was apparently written in Japanese, though the oldest surviving edition is in Chinese.

Dai-Nihon Hokke Genki, as the name implies, is a collection of stories intended primarily to inspire faith in the Lotus Sutra and the miracles this sutra was responsible for in Japan. The work is written in Chinese and its readership was probably limited to monks. Presumably they would have retold the stories in Japanese using the collection as a source book for sermons rather than as a text. It contains one hundred twenty-nine tales and is organized into three volumes. Usually ascribed to the monk Chingen, the work's compilation date is reckoned to be some time between 1040 and 1043.

Hokke Genki was an important source for *Konjaku,* especially for those tales included in *Konjaku's* volume XII (ten stories), Volume XIII (forty-one stories), and XIV (twenty-one stories).[22] These *Konjaku* volumes, it will be seen, contain tales of praise for the wonders of the Lotus Sutra. *Hokke Genki* is also thought to be the source for thirteen of the tales in volume XV, a volume containing stories about people reborn in the Western Paradise of Amida, a fact which underscores how deeply these two beliefs (the Lotus Sutra and Amida's Paradise) were inter-connected in Heian Japan. In any event, well over half of the tales in *Hokke Genki* have found their way into *Konjaku Monogatari-shū.*

There is a difference in the type of hero found in *Hokke Genki* from that found in earlier works such as *Ryōiki,* which is worth noting partly because it seems to have some impact on *Konjaku.* The hero of the typical *Hokke Genki* story is often a "seeker of truth," a person who, as a devotee of the Lotus Sutra, has undergone an intensely personal religious experience. The tales in *Ryōiki* feature mainly immediate retribution and thus are more concerned with punishments and rewards than with devotion.

Since the *Konjaku* compiler places a great deal of emphasis on the "true heartedness" of his heroes and often comments on the importance of sincerity, it seems entirely possible that he was impressed with this aspect of the *Hokke Genki* heroes and took more from this work than its stories. Certainly *Hokke Genki* is a work which deserves more study in both Japan and the West.

Hyakuza Hōdan Kikigaki-shō was only discovered fairly recently and is not very well known, even in Japan. It is of considerable value to those who are interested in how stories were transmitted and in the content of the ceremonies conducted for aristocratic Buddhists, for it is a bare-boned outline of the sermons delivered by the preachers at a large ceremony for the Lotus Sutra which was held at the temple Daian-ji beginning on the eighteenth day of the second month of 1110.

The text of *Hyakuza* is thought to have been completed soon after the ceremony itself—which was originally scheduled for one hundred days but eventually lengthened to three hundred—was over. The identity of the sponsor of the ceremony is still a matter of conjecture; all that is known is that the sponsor was a princess who had a pious interest in Buddhism. This and all other information we have about the ceremony is what can be gleaned from the work itself.

The *Hyakuza* text as it now exists includes twenty entries, nearly all of which contain at least one story. There is very little development of narrative in these sections, however. The speakers vary, and their names are usually mentioned in the text. The Hossō, Kegon, and Tendai sects appear to be represented but this is also a matter of conjecture and is still being debated. The tales

draw on incidents from India, China, and Japan and are interspersed with commentaries from sutras as well as direct comments
by the speakers. Although it is unlikely that the tales were told
in the exact form they appear in the written texts—we must
assume that they were more elaborate and that the scribes were
unable to take them down word for word—the text as a whole
gives us a good picture of the actual working of a Buddhist
ceremony. I find it particularly important that there are tales set
in India, for this might indicate that *Konjaku*'s Indian tales, too,
were widely used in actual preaching situations.

We can get some idea of the method employed by the *Hyakuza*
preachers by comparing a story found there with a variant of the
same tale as it is told by the *Konjaku* compiler. The *Hyakuza* tale
was told on the ninth day of the third month in 1110 and relates
how although a school of fish approaches an island, the inhabitants
of the island are unable to catch any of these fish in their nets.
Finally one fisherman loses his patience and exclaims, "Namu
Amida Butsu!"—apparently as an oath rather than as a pious
invocation of Amida—and the fish begin to swim to him, al-
lowing themselves to be taken up in his nets. All of the villagers
then adopt this method and soon they have made a good catch.

It is explained by the preacher that *Namu Amida Butsu* (literally,
"Praise to Amida Buddha") happens to be the name of this particular species of fish and that the fish came to the villagers
because they felt a trust for them when they heard their names
called. The narrator ends by informing us that as a result of
having chanted the name of Amida—even though not from a
religious feeling—the villagers were all granted long lives and
were all reborn in the Western Paradise when they finally did
die.

As it is found in *Konjaku* this tale differs considerably. It is
placed with the Indian stories (IV.37) and is told more as a story
about Amida himself than about salvation in general. In the
Konjaku version the fish themselves chant "Namu Amida Butsu"
and the fishermen imitate them. At this point the fish allow
themselves to be caught. The fishermen further discover that the
fish taste better when more people have chanted the name, so

the result is that most of the villagers spend most of their time chanting the holy name.

A villager then dies and reappears to the living villagers, telling them that the fish were in fact Amida himself. Because he felt sorry for the villagers' ignorance of Buddhism, Amida transformed himself into the fish so that he could induce the people to chant his name and save themselves.

It is likely that both the *Konjaku* compiler and the *Hyakuza* narrator had the same Chinese source for their separate versions of this tale but the *Hyakuza* version is geared toward an audience meant to be impressed and set on the right track. The *Konjaku* version fits nicely into the overall scheme of volume IV, which contains stories about the disciples of Buddha after his death. The *Konjaku* story seems much less likely to succeed with a listening audience, aimed as it is at readers. The *Hyakuza* story inspires faith in the power of Amida and the mere chanting of his name, while the *Konjaku* story stresses his virtue rather than his power. The *Hyakuza* version is clearly the more didactic of the two.

Uchigiki-shū is a collection of twenty-seven stories and is incomplete in its present form. It is something like *Hyakuza* in that it has close ties to sermons of preachers but it is more a retelling of the stories than an outline account as we find in *Hyakuza*. The date of the oldest hand-copied manuscript is 1134, so it is speculated that *Uchigiki* must have been produced shortly before that time.[23] The authorship is unknown, though it seems likely that the compiler was a monk connected with the Tendai sect.

Twenty-one of the twenty-seven stories in *Uchigiki* have either a direct or indirect connection with *Konjaku Monogatari-shū*, and although it does not appear that either collection borrowed directly from the other, it is significant that three-fourths of the tales from this collection of sermons have found their way into *Konjaku*. If both collections were the work of Tendai monks who were active as preachers, the large number of tales in common would be easily understandable.

The *Konjaku* narratives are fuller and have more elaboration
and detail, a fact which is understandable if indeed the *Uchigiki*
stories were taken down in some kind of shorthand as they were
delivered by a preacher. We will examine some of the similarities
and differences of the narrative styles of these two works below.

Collections Intended for Entertainment. It should not be
thought that all *setsuwa* collections were inspired by Buddhism
and bound up in its needs. We know, for example, of the existence
of at least one secular tale collection from fragments which have
been found,[24] and doubtless there were others as well. I will
discuss only two collections here, both of which have close ties
to *Konjaku Monogatari-shū*. These are *Kohon Setsuwa-shū* and *Uji
Shūi Monogatari*. Both of these works are very important in the
history of *setsuwa* literature, but it should also be noted that they
are not the only collections intended primarily for entertainment.[25]

Kohon Setsuwa-shū is a collection of seventy stories in two volumes; it was discovered in 1943. Its manuscript was wrapped in
paper bearing the name "Konjaku Monogatari," and it had the
seal of a collector from the early Meiji period. The fact that it
was called "Konjaku Monogatari" is ample evidence of the close
relationship between these two collections. It is likely that they
were both produced about the same time, though we know virtually nothing about either the compiler or date of *Kohon*. The
title is a makeshift one supplied by modern scholars.

Kohon contains about forty parallels with *Konjaku* stories, but
it does not appear that either borrowed directly from the other.
Kohon's first volume contains mostly poem-tale types of stories
and the second mostly popular Buddhist tales. The presence of
both kinds of stories in this one work is intriguing because it
demonstrates that the Buddhist, prosaic *setsuwa* were understood
by the Heian aristocrats as having a good deal in common with
the most aesthetic poem tales.

Kohon has been compared to *Ōkagami*, a historical romance,
and even to *Genji Monogatari*, the best known of the romances
produced in the Heian court.[26] The importance of this work in

the overall history of Japanese literature has yet to be adequately gauged.

Next to *Konjaku*, *Uji Shūi Monogatari* is the best known of the *setsuwa* collections. It contains 197 stories and is generally considered to date from the early thirteenth century. Its compiler is unknown. Some forty-three tales found in *Uji Shūi* are also found in *Konjaku*, though it is unlikely that there has been any direct borrowing. Most scholars postulate an intermediate work of some sort between the two; the logical candidate for this honor is the elusive *Uji Dainagon Monogatari*. *Konjaku*, *Kohon*, and *Uji Shūi* contain a number of stories in common and form one of the more perplexing triangles in the study of Japanese literature.

The language of *Uji Shūi* is pure Japanese and probably closer to the spoken language of the day than either *Konjaku* or the romances of the court. Its style is brisk and less detailed than that of *Konjaku;* apparently the compiler had entertainment in mind rather than any didactic purpose and thus pared his tales to make for easy reading. The stories are both Buddhist and secular and cover India, China, and Japan, but there is no particular division as to geography or subject matter such as we have seen in *Konjaku*. Basically, the tales appear to be arranged in an arbitrary manner.

Collections Made for the Salvation of the Compiler. I have devised this rather imprecise category to cover some of the later collections which, although mainly Buddhist in content, do not seem to have any particular connections with preaching or sermons. Rather, they appear to have been put together because of the compiler's desire to associate himself with the holy stories and were meant to further the compiler's good works, thus aiding in his own salvation. Although most of the collections in this group are relatively late and are associated with religious hermits, the group does contain one quite early collection, *Nihon Ōjō Gokuraku-ki.* Two other major collections that fall in this category are *Senjūshō* and *Hosshin-shū,* both of which have been attributed to famous poet-monks.

Nihon Ōjō Gokuraku-ki is the first known work in a subgenre of tales known as *ōjō den,* or biographies of people who were reborn in the Western Paradise. It is in all likelihood the first of these works, as it begins with the tale of Prince Regent Shōtoku, who is credited with having introduced Buddhism to Japan. It contains forty-five biographies and was used fairly extensively by the *Konjaku* compiler, mostly in volume XV, which contains similar stories.

The author of *Gokuraku-ki* was Yoshishige no Yasutane (d. 997), who is the hero of *Konjaku* XIX.3. Yasutane died after a fairly distinguished career as an Imperial Scribe; he was also an ardent Buddhist and was associated with Genshin during his lifetime. *Gokuraku-ki* was written about 980, and the major reason for its production was Yasutane's desire to associate himself with the holy stories it contained. He was a member of a group of people who had pledged to assist each other in any way in the attainment of salvation in Amida's Paradise, and these people were in the habit of attending the deaths of those who were particularly holy in hopes that some of the merit of the dying person would be transferred to the living.

In short, any type of association with rebirth in the Western Paradise was considered to be something of great individual merit, and collections such as Yasutane's were seen as extremely valuable works. There are six such collections extant. Parenthetically it might be noted that in the second extant work in this group there is a story about Yasutane, so we can assume that his efforts were of some use to him.

The stories in the *ōjō den* follow a general formula: first they name the person, then give his teacher's name if he was a monk (or his lay background if he was not); they then mention his religious devotional practices (usually a combination of chanting the name of Amida and devotion to the Lotus Sutra), and finally they relate the circumstances of his death and the attendant miracles which reveal his successful rebirth. In the later collections we have an increasing number of unnamed heroes. The tales are basically thumbnail sketches and were used by the *Konjaku* compiler for their information rather than for plot or wording.

The traditional date for *Senjūshō,* a collection of 103 tales, is 1183, but it could have been compiled as late as 1258. The work is traditionally attributed to the poet-monk Saigyō (1118–1190), one of Japan's most famous hermits, but there is no consensus that he was indeed the compiler. It is generally thought now that Saigyō may have been responsible for some of the stories in the collection but not for its compilation as a whole. The style of this work is very ornate and it contains many poems, but the theme of renouncing the world and leading a religious life is predominant throughout the collection.

To show some of the significant differences between this work and *Konjaku* one need only compare the image of the holy man Zōga as it is drawn in each work. There are many different treatments of Zōga in various *setsuwa* collections and most of the stories told about him can also be found in *Konjaku.* The *Senjūshō* treatment of this monk contains a story (the first story in the collection) of how he prayed earnestly at the shrine of the Sun Goddess at Ise for enlightenment and was instructed to cast off all thoughts of fame and profit in this world. This he did by giving away all his clothes, apparently reasoning that his body was not important enough to cover, and walking back to Mt. Hiei, an act which created quite a stir. The *Senjūshō* compiler, whoever he may have been, praises Zōga lavishly for this act. The incident is not recorded in *Konjaku Monogatari-shū.*

Although Zōga was not particularly symbolic of the new Buddhism to the compiler of *Konjaku,* it would seem that he had attained that status by the time of the compilation of *Senjūshō:* the story of Zōga is the first tale in *Senjūshō.* The *Senjūshō* compiler was particularly impressed by this absolute dedication to the religious life and many of his stories reflect this attraction.

It should also be noted that the compiler of *Senjūshō* took a great deal of interest in the stories he collected and wrote extensive commentaries on them. Indeed, in many of the tales there is more commentary than narrative. In the Zōga story, for example, the mercy of the Sun Goddess is lauded along with many other things. All in all, the tone of this collection is much more personal than the tone of works such as *Uchigiki-shū.*

Hosshin-shū, which is dated about 1215, is also attributed to a famous poet-monk, in this case Kamo no Chōmei (1153–1216), who is most famous for his work *Hōjōki* [An Account of My Hut], a short essay on the joys of his withdrawal from the world. *Hosshin-shū* contains one hundred two tales and like *Senjūshō* its main theme is the renunciation of the world and the taking up of the religious life. The stories in *Hosshin-shū* are written in a simpler, more direct style than those of *Senjūshō* and there is considerably less commentary on the tales. The narrative style is not very polished, Chōmei having put more energy into his selections than into his narrative.

The compiler of a work produced at about the same time (*Kankyo no Tomo,* about 1222) gives us an insight into Chōmei and his motives for compiling a collection of *setsuwa.* According to *Kankyo no Tomo,* "Chōmei delights the ear and at the same time he establishes *kechien.*" The word *kechien* is a difficult one to translate; essentially it means that Chōmei has established a bond of holiness between himself and his listeners or readers through the sacred nature of the stories he has transmitted. This is in the tradition established by people like Yoshishige no Yasutane, the compiler of the first of the *ōjō den,* who had as their main concern their own rebirth in the Western Paradise of Amida.

The above is by no means a complete listing of the various *setsuwa* collections; it would also be possible to devise wholly different categories for collections. What I have attempted to do here is to identify and define three main currents in the general stream of *setsuwa* literature so that we might come to a better understanding of the place of *Konjaku Monogatari-shū.* It should be stressed that the placing of a work in one category does not mean that it has none of the characteristics of collections in the other two categories. No collection is totally without entertainment value, for example, and works which were concerned with salvation in general held interest for both audience and compiler.

Let us now look at *Konjaku,* comparing its stories with those of collections from the various categories, and see where this work fits into the genre.

Konjaku Monogatari-shū as a *Setsuwa* Collection

The connection between *Konjaku* and the works I have placed in my third category—those collections which were made with the salvation of the compiler as the primary goal—is somewhat tenuous. This is not to say that there is no connection at all, for clearly *Konjaku* has used a good number of tales from *Nihon Ōjō Gokuraku-ki,* for example. Only eight items from the 102 in *Hosshin-shū* have parallels in *Konjaku.*[27] By the same token, some fifteen of the *Hosshin-shū* stories have parallels in one or another of the *ōjō den,* a fact which demonstrates the basic affinity between these collections.

If we look at the types of stories common to *Hosshin-shū* and *Konjaku,* moreover, we will find that the story which attracted both compilers was generally one of two types—stories about people who have made complete commitments to a religious way of life and stories which contain poems.

The large number of parallels between *Konjaku* and *Gokuraku-ki* is easily explained when we remember that faith in the Western Paradise of Amida was, after all, a key element in Heian Buddhism, and was clearly important to the *Konjaku* compiler, and *Gokuraku-ki* was one of his most convenient sources for tales of this sort.

The next question we must ask is how *Konjaku* relates to collections in the first and second groups—those which were concerned primarily with the salvation and entertainment of their readers. This is a difficult question and there is no totally satisfactory answer to it, but I think the evidence indicates that *Konjaku* has more affinity with the stories in the first group than those of the second.

To investigate this problem it is necessary to outline the relationship between *Konjaku Monogatari-shū* and three other collections. The three are *Uji Shūi Monogatari, Kohon Setsuwa-shū,* and *Uchigiki-shū.* (For the sake of convenience I will refer to these collections as *USM*, *KHS*, and *UGS* below.) It has been recognized that there is a fascinating interdependence among these four collections since the existence of *KHS* came to light in 1943. The precise nature of the relationships, however, is still a matter of some debate, with opinions varying particularly on the question of the relationship between *Konjaku* and *UGS*.

There are twenty tales[28] that appear in at least three of these four collections. All of these tales are in *Konjaku* but none appears in all four collections. All other possibilities for combinations— *Konjaku, KHS, USM; Konjaku, KHS, UGS;* and *Konjaku, UGS, USM*—do exist, however, giving us the opportunity to examine relative treatments of the stories and to classify *Konjaku* on the basis of its affinities with other collections. I will examine these group by group below.

Stories in *Konjaku*, *USM*, and *KHS*.   This is the largest of the three groups, containing a total of fourteen separate stories. These are as follows:

Konjaku	USM	KHS
3.22	85	56
14.35	191	52
16.6	87	64
16.7	108	54
16.28	96	58
16.30	131	59
16.37	86	57
17.47	192	61
19.11	89.	69
19.13	148	40
19.40	95	49
24.43	149	41
24.55	111	44
27.2	151	27

There is no readily apparent pattern in the order in which the tales appear in various collections, and one must assume that the position of the tales in each collection has been fixed by each of the three different compilers for individual reasons.[29]

What can be said with confidence, however, is that the stories used in *USM* and *KHS* tend to be more similar to each other than they are to the variants in *Konjaku*. As other scholars have also observed, this holds true for nearly every tale in this group,[30] and I will discuss only two story sets here.

The first is *Konjaku* XIX. 11, which has parallels in *USM* 89 and *KHS* 69. The title of this story is "The Conversion of the Watō Kannon in Shinano Province" ("Watō" is read "Batō" in *USM*). An old man living near certain hot springs famous for their medicinal powers has a dream in which he is informed that the Kannon, the Bodhisattva of Mercy, will visit the springs the following day in the form of a hunter who had injured his arm. The old man is given a complete description of the hunter. He informs all the people of the area and they purify the place and await the visit. When a man answering the description arrives, everyone begins worshiping, much to the man's consternation. He eventually determines the reason for the excitement and on the spot decides to cut off his hair and become a monk. He goes off to Mt. Hiei to study for a time, then disappears.

This basic plot is followed in all three of the collections, and there are places where the wording is almost exactly the same in all three, but there are indications that the *Konjaku* version stands apart from the other two. For example, the man is said by the *Konjaku* compiler to have broken his left arm, but in *USM* and *KHS* it is his right arm. Further, *USM* and *KHS* both put the man's age at about thirty years, but *Konjaku* makes it forty.

Two passages where the wording is different bear examination, if only briefly. The first of these is the passage which describes the reactions of the residents of the hot springs area when the hero appears. In *USM* there is the following passage:

All of the people quickly stood, then prostrated themselves, touching the ground with their foreheads. This man was considerably surprised, not understanding what they were doing. He asked them, but all were offering prayer after prayer and no one would tell him anything.

The passage in *KHS* is exactly the same, with no changes in wording at all. In *Konjaku*, however, it reads as follows:

He faced all these people and asked, "What is going on here?" but nobody told him; all were worshiping.

It seems obvious that the *Konjaku* compiler or a scribe somewhere in the transmission process overlooked a line in the original text, for the man's question makes no sense in the context of the *Konjaku* tale. In order to understand the question we need the information supplied in the *USM* and *KHS* versions that all present began to worship when the man arrived.

We will find more than mistakes in copying that mark *Konjaku* as differing from the other two works, however. Consider the following passage, the description of the point when the man determines to cut off his hair and become a monk. In *USM* we have the following:

The man was perplexed, and decided that he really was the Kannon. So he decided to become a monk, and discarding his bow, arrows, and swords, he became a monk.

The *KHS* version is virtually identical:

The man was perplexed and decided that he really was the Kannon. So he decided to become a monk, and taking off his bow, arrows, and swords, he became a monk.

In *Konjaku,* however, we have a slightly different version:

Perplexed, the man said, "Then my person must be a Kannon. Well, this same body will become a monk." And right there in the garden he discarded his bow and arrows, threw away his warrior's staff, cut off his topknot, and without further ado became a monk.

The *USM* and *KHS* versions are both indirect. I have rendered the verb *omofu* as "decided" here while some might choose to render the passage in quotation marks as a direct thought, but in either case these two versions deal with the man's thoughts and not with his actual actions as the *Konjaku* compiler does. The *Konjaku* version is, as a result, a more dramatic one. In *Konjaku* the conversion is the focal point of the story, but both *USM* and *KHS* seem to lack this focal point. If the first passage I discussed could be attributed to a mistake in copying, this one is obviously a conscious alteration by the *Konjaku* compiler.

One more example of the differences in narrative style should suffice to show how *Konjaku* stands slightly apart from the other two collections in this group. This story is *Konjaku* XIX. 13 (*USM* 148 and *KHS* 40), a tale about the retainer of a high-ranking aristocrat who distinguishes himself with a skillful poem when his master rather cruelly asks for one; the man then takes the robes he has been awarded for his poem and gives them to a holy man in payment for the holy man's administering of the Buddhist vows to him.

After the man is awarded the robes the *USM* version reads:

Then, this attendant was not seen afterwards. The governor thought this strange and had a search conducted, and they found that he had gone off to a holy man living in the mountains to the north. He had taken the two robes he had received and said . . .

The *KHS* version is similar:

Then, this man was not seen for three days and thinking this strange the governor had a search conducted. They found that he had gone off to a wondrous holy man living in a holy temple in the mountains to the north. He had taken the two robes he had received and said . . .

Once again the *Konjaku* compiler has made significant changes:

After this the attendant was not seen for two or three days and when the governor heard about his absence he was suspicious, and had people inquire after him, but they were unable to find any trace of him at all.

"He has taken those robes and fled," the governor thought, doubting the man's intentions, but in fact, in the mountains north of the governor's mansion there was a holy mountain temple called [   ], where there was a worthy holy man. The attendant had gone to pay his respects to this holy man and had given him the two robes he had received, with the words . . .

There are two points that could be made about these passages if we wish to understand *Konjaku* in terms of the other two collections. First, the *Konjaku* compiler felt compelled, as he often did, to name the temple. The lacuna was probably left intentionally with the idea of checking on the information at a later date. This is typical of *Konjaku* and indicates that the compiler was trying to educate his readers; the *USM* and *KHS* compilers, on the other hand, were more in the business of entertainment and omitted detail which was unimportant in their eyes.

The second concerns *Konjaku*'s attempts to make a more dramatic narrative style. In this case the compiler describes the man's actions partly from the perspective of the governor, setting up an opposition which increases the dramatic affect of the passage. In addition to this, the man's actions are seen as even more holy in light of the governor's suspicions.

Differences such as those cited above can be seen in greater or lesser degree in almost all of the stories which *Konjaku* shares with *USM* and *KHS*. It seems clear that the *Konjaku* compiler had different concerns from the compilers of these two collections and approached his material accordingly. When we remember that the primary purpose of *USM* and *KHS* is entertainment, we can assume that the *Konjaku* compiler had some purpose beyond entertainment in mind when he went about his editorial work. The large number of stories from both these collections which are also found in *Konjaku*—somewhere around half of the totals of each work have *Konjaku* parallels—tells us, however, that the compiler certainly did not hesitate in choosing stories he thought would be entertaining.

Stories in *Konjaku*, *KHS*, and *UGS*.   There are only two stories in this group, a fact that is not surprising if we remember how different *UGS* and *KHS* are in function. The stories are as follows:

Konjaku	KHS	UGS
4.24	63	13
14.42	51	23

As was the case in the first group, there is little doubt about the interpretation of the evidence here. In both cases the *Konjaku* version tends to be closer to the *UGS* tale than it is to the *KHS* story.

In the case of *Konjaku* IV.24, for example, Takahashi Mitsugu finds thirteen places where the wording is similar in *Konjaku* and *UGS* and fairly different from that of *KHS*. Conversely, he finds only six places where *Konjaku* and *KHS* seem to be more alike. These six places, furthermore, are minor and do nothing to affect the story, while some of the thirteen are important to the tale. *Konjaku* and *UGS* agree on numbers, with *KHS* disagreeing, and the same can be said about the use of proper names in the stories.[31]

This is such a small grouping that its value as evidence is limited, but we can see nonetheless that *Konjaku* has here a closer affinity with a collection of sermon notes than it does to *KHS*, which was a collection intended primarily for entertainment.

Stories in *Konjaku*, *USM*, and *UGS*. We come, then, to the last and most perplexing of the possible combinations. There are four stories in this group:

Konjaku	USM	UGS
5.31	171	20
6.1	195	2
9.13	164	21
11.11	170	18

If the pattern established by the first two groupings—*Konjaku* having more affinity with a collection of sermon notes than with a collection of entertaining tales—were to hold true we would expect to find clear-cut evidence that *Konjaku* is closer to *UGS* than it is to *USM*. This is precisely the result arrived at by Takahashi Mitsugu,[32] but unfortunately it is not so overwhelming as he would have us believe. D. E. Mills, in fact, comes to the opposite conclusion, stating that, "in the stories common to all three, the wording of *Uchigiki* is on the whole closer to that of *Uji Shūi* than to that of *Konjaku*."[33]

A close examination of the stories leads me to believe that it is virtually impossible to say with any degree of confidence at all that any one collection is "closer" to one of the two than it is to the other. Takahashi finds a clear-cut case in the example of *Konjaku* XI.11 (*USM* 170, *UGS* 18); in this story there are ten places where the wording of *Konjaku* and *UGS* is similar and different from that of *USM*, and only two cases where *Konjaku* and *USM* differ from *UGS*. Further, there are other places where the *Uji Shūi* compiler has apparently added expressions not in either *Konjaku* or *Uchigiki*.[34] It is only in this single tale, however, where the distinctions are obvious.

Takahashi also considers the case of *Konjaku* V.31 (*USM* 171, *UGS* 20), the story of a monk who goes through a hole in a mountain and enters a new world where he eats some flowers only to find that they make him grow so large that he is now unable to return to his own world through the hole he used as an entryway, as being another case of the pairing of *Konjaku* and *UGS*.[35] He admits that all three tales in this case are substantially different from one another and that *Konjaku* in particular presents a unique treatment of the story which was probably influenced by oral tradition. According to Takahashi, however, in the two places where the wording of the three collections is similar *Konjaku* corresponds to the *UGS* treatment rather than to the *USM* version. The fact that there are only three places where the wording corresponds at all in the three collections makes it difficult to compare the three, however, and we must be cautious about accepting Takahashi's results in this case.

On the other hand, Mills finds that in the case of *Konjaku* VI.1 (*USM* 195, *UGS* 2), the *UGS* and *USM* versions are closer to each other than they are to *Konjaku*.[36]

The final tale in this group, *Konjaku* IX.13 (*USM* 164, *UGS* 21), presents a situation that is even more perplexing than the three discussed above. Mills holds that *USM* and *UGS* in this case "resemble each other more then *Konjaku*,"[37] but I believe that this is another instance where it is impossible to come to any conclusion. The tale presents several formidable problems, and one would have to conclude that there is no one version that is clearly unique when compared to the other two.

Conclusion. Where, then, does this leave us in our attempt to classify *Konjaku Monogatari-shū* on the basis of its relationships with other *setsuwa* collections? The lack of a clear conclusion in the final grouping is frustrating, because it does not complete a pattern which had been set in the first two groups. The theory— that *Konjaku* is a collection used in preaching and therefore should be closer to other such collections than to collections used for entertainment—is an enticing one, and Takahashi, for one, seems to have been interpreting his evidence to fit the theory even though the evidence does not always lend itself to such an interpretation.

On the other hand, we cannot conclude that the theory is incorrect. At least twenty of the twenty-seven stories in *Uchigiki-shū* have parallels in *Konjaku,* a fact that demonstrates undeniably that these two collections are closely related. *Uchigiki* is a relatively small collection and the actual number of tales involved is lower than is the case with *Kohon Setsuwa-shū* and *Uji Shūi Monogatari,* but it is still instructive to compare the percentages involved. A much higher percentatge of the tales in *UGS* appear in *Konjaku* than is the case with either *USM* or *KHS*.

We can say that the *Konjaku* compiler consistently selected tales of the sermon variety but he also took great care to use stories which would be attractive to an aristocratic audience. This observation is borne out by comparing *Konjaku*'s use of stories also appearing in *KHS* and *USM*. The *Kohon* tales have on the whole more traditional aesthetic appeal than do the *Uji Shūi* stories, and a higher percentage of these *Kohon* tales appear in *Konjaku* than is the case with the *Uji Shūi* stories. The *Konjaku* compiler made changes in this aristocratic group of tales to suit his didactic Buddhist purposes.

On the other hand, he also made certain changes in the sermon-type tales which appear in *Uchigiki-shū;* these are by and large consistent with his general style of narrative. The logical conclusion would appear to be that *Konjaku* is a collection which belongs with those collections of sermon material such as *Ryōiki,*

Uchigiki, Hyakuza and the like, but that its compiler took special
care to insure that his tales would appeal to a wide group of
people, and especially to aristocrats.

Konjaku is not a collection of sermons, but is a collection of
stories suitable for sermons. The compiler has given the individual
monk who might use his collection much material to work with
but has not gone so far as to define the material overmuch. His
conclusions, for example, could be used or not used, depending
on the occasion of the sermon; the stories in the first ten volumes
are useful primarily as background but also might have been
utilized in a sermon; and the encyclopedic arrangement of the
tales would have been very useful to the preacher, for it would
have made it simple to find an appropriate tale for any given
topic.

Given all these characteristics, it is no surprise that *Konjaku
Monogatari-shū* occupies such an important spot in the history of
setsuwa literature, for there is something in it to attract the compiler of any other type of tale collection. Let us now turn to a
more detailed description of the collection.

Chapter Three
The Compiler's Vision

Konjaku Monogatari-shū is composed of thirty-one volumes (*maki,* literally "scroll"), and must have contained upwards of 1,100 tales in its original form, provided that it was ever completed. In all present texts volumes VIII, XVIII, and XXI are missing, as are many individual stories within the various volumes, and the work as we have it today contains a total of 1,039 stories. Some of these are incomplete.

In this chapter I will describe the contents of the collections mainly through discussion of tales which I will translate, so that the reader may have the opportunity to experience the stories directly, but it should be stressed that it is impossible to select four "representative" tales from 1,039, and that some amount of summary and indirect presentation will be necessary as well. Before embarking on this description, however, I would like to present some additional background.

Konjaku draws its name from the fact that all of its stories begin with the phrase *ima wa mukashi,* or "long ago," and the Chinese characters used to write these two words can also be read *kon* and *jaku,* respectively, due to the fact that when the Japanese borrowed characters from China they adapted them not only for their meanings, but also assigned each character a reading which was a Japanese imitation of the original Chinese sound value. The *monogatari* of the title means "story," and *shū* means "collection," so the title could be translated into English as "A Collection of Tales of Long Ago."

Some understanding of the Japanese scripts is helpful in approaching *Konjaku.* The Japanese eventually standardized certain of the Chinese characters into phonetic scripts so that they could either express their language in a written form which was entirely phonetic, or in one which combined the Chinese characters with the scripts, employing the characters for their meanings and the script to express the sound changes which occur in inflected languages such as Japanese, grammatical particles and the like. Two such scripts were actually devised—*katakana* was used mostly in official documents and to express the Japanized Chinese readings of difficult characters, and *hiragana*, a cursive script, was used on more informal occasions such as the writing of native Japanese poetry and in love notes passed between women and men.

Hiragana, being phonetic, was relatively easy to learn and was used by women, who generally were not educated in Chinese and who did not use the more "masculine" *katakana*.

It is a well-known fact that a great deal of the literature of the Heian period, including the masterpiece *Tale of Genji,* was written phonetically in *hiragana* by women. This is often explained by the theory that women, being illiterate in Chinese, were free to write more expressively in their own language, but that men were constrained and unable to express themselves gracefully in Chinese, which was, after all, a foreign language.

A serious problem with this explanation is the fact that men did use *hiragana* and Japanese. Furthermore, there exist works of literature written in perfectly expressive Japanese with a mixture of *katakana* and Chinese characters.

The best example of this is *Konjaku Monogatari-shū.* Its stories are written primarily in Chinese characters, with only verb endings and grammatical particles expressed in *katakana,* and for this reason we can assume that the compiler was a male. The language of *Konjaku* is, for all its use of Chinese characters, fairly close to the colloquial language and most of its stories would have been perfectly intelligible when read aloud.

The Levels of Organization

The most obvious level of organization present in *Konjaku Monogatari-shū* is, as I have noted, geographical. The first five of the collection's volumes contain stories set in India, the second five contain tales set in China, and the remaining tales are set in Japan. This, of course, mirrors the spread of Buddhism, which went to China from India, and then came to Japan somewhat later.

After the geographical organization there is what I will call the obvious organization by subject matter. That is to say, tales are either Buddhist or secular, and are so labeled by the compiler. All of the Indian tales are Buddhist, as are volumes VI to IX in the Chinese section and XI to XX in the Japanese.

This, however, represents only one tier of the subject matter type of organization; there is also a much more detailed plan to be found in each of the four (Indian, Chinese, Japanese Buddhist, and Japanese secular) major divisions of the collection. This more detailed plan was first discovered by Kunisaki Funimaro, and it is to his ideas that we must now turn our attention.[1]

According to Kunisaki, the tales in each of these divisions are arranged in groups: first there are stories about history, then stories of praise, and finally didactic stories. The tales he classifies as praise in the Buddhist sections are concerned with the so-called "three treasures" of Buddhism—the Buddha, the law (*dharma*), and the *samgha,* or the community of monks. The didactic tales are specific interpretations of events in this world according to the Buddhist ideas of cause and effect, or the concept that what happens in the present world takes place because of our actions in the past. The "past" in this case can refer either to one's current or previous existences.

There is yet another Buddhist concept which is important to an understanding of the organization of tales in *Konjaku Monogatari-shū*, and this is the idea of the stages of transmission of the Buddhist law following the death of the historical Buddha. According to a theory popular in Japan and China, the true teaching of Buddha could be transmitted accurately for a period of only a thousand years after his death, and after that time the world would enter a second stage, a time when the true doctrine would continue to be transmitted but would be confused with many false doctrines which would also spring up. These first two stages are know in Japan as *shōbō* and *zōbō,* or the periods of true transmission and of the transmission of many falsehoods.

The third and final stage is one called *mappō;* it was interpreted by the Japanese as beginning two thousand years after the death of Buddha. This was thought to be a period in which the true doctrine would disappear completely, making it impossible for an individual to attain enlightenment on his own merits. This period had begun by the time *Konjaku* was completed, and it is worth noting that it coincided with a time of social instability in the nation, a fact which doubtless made Buddhist truth seem all the more real to Japanese Buddhists. There are many references to the "latter days of the law" (*mappō*) in *Konjaku*.

This was likely a central organizing principle behind *Konjaku* because it accounts for the difference in emphases found in the Indian stories, the Chinese stories, and the Japanese stories.

The Indian tales, for example, describe the acts of Buddha and his immediate followers, and stress the virtue of self-sacrifice. Self-sacrifice is also described in some of the Chinese tales, but it seems to be a rapidly disappearing virtue when compared with the Indian stories. The Chinese didactic tales, in particular, tend to focus on the punishments meted out to those who do not follow Buddhist laws; there is obviously more need to show wrong acts in the Chinese context, for wrong acts would have been much easier to commit in the age of *zōbō*. As for the Japanese stories, we find that once the world has entered the stage of *mappō* the question is no longer really one of right and wrong so much as it is one of placing one's faith in the power of Amida or the Lotus Sutra, and acknowledging that one's own powers are insufficient for salvation.

This same general pattern can be seen in the tales of praise as well as in the didactic stories. Stories in praise of the Buddha in the India sections deal with the man himself, while those in the Chinese section are about his image. There are, of course, also tales about images of Buddha in the Japanese Buddhist section, but it is important to note that statistically the Japanese stories of praise contain a much higher percentage of tales about Bodhisattvas, those noble people who have refused to enter nirvana until all living beings have been saved, than they do stories about the image of Buddha.

In brief, the compiler of *Konjaku* seems to have believed that the quality of reality had dropped sharply from the days of Buddha to his own times, and he therefore found it necessary to deal increasingly with symbols rather than the real thing. By the time we get to Japan in this collection man is seen as thoroughly helpless, needing to give his entire life over to sincere entreaties for assistance to those powerful symbols such as Amida, Kannon (the Bodhisattva of Mercy), and the Lotus Sutra.

Thus when one speaks of the theme of *Konjaku* one must be careful to specify what section of the collection one is talking about, for the themes differ from section to section. The major theme of the Indian stories is the idea of self-sacrifice and individual attainment as practiced by the Buddha, while the major theme of the Chinese tales might be said to be the power of Buddha. When we get to the Japanese Buddhist stories, the major theme is the necessity to dedicate one's life to religious pursuits, and the tales describe a large number of people who have done just that, relying on Buddhist symbols because they recognize that their own strength is not sufficient.

The Japanese secular tales have a slightly different theme, though it is one which is compatible with that of the Japanese Buddhist stories. Roughly stated, these tales concentrate on the importance of dedication and a quick wit for those who wish to make it successfully through the world. The ability to distinguish reality from illusion, or truth from falsehood, was of the highest importance to the compiler, and this motif helps to unify the different sections, each of which presents a slightly different reality.

In the following discussion I explore each of the four major sections of the work, using as a springboard in each case a story which seems to me to be more or less representative. It would be impossible to give a full indication of the richness of subject matter found in *Konjaku* without using a considerably larger number of tales, but these should serve as an introduction.

The Indian Stories

Let us begin with a consideration of V.8, "How King Daikō Myōō gave his head to a fortune teller."

Long ago there was a king in India known as King Daikō Myōō. Moved to give away his possessions to people, he loaded five hundred elephants with various treasures, then gathered a large number of people together and gave the treasures to them, not regretting the loss even the slightest bit. Needless to say, if a person came and asked for something he would never refuse.

The king of the neighboring country heard about this and in order to kill King Daikō Myōō, he hired a fortuneteller, instructing him to go to King Daikō Myōō and ask for his head. The fortuneteller went to the king and was about to make his request but the deity guarding the palace knew about it and alerted the palace guards, who would not let the fortuneteller in the palace gates. A palace guard told the king what had happened, however. The king came out and looked at the fortuneteller with as trusting a look as a child might give its mother. Rejoicing in his heart, the king asked the reason for the visit. The fortuneteller said, "I have come to ask for the king's head."

The king replied, "In accordance with your request, I will present you with my head," acceding to the demand. First he went into the inner palace to face his queens and his five hundred imperial princes and tell them of the fortuneteller's request for his head.

When the queens and the imperial princes heard this they all fell to the ground prostrate with grief and tried very hard to change his mind. The king was determined, however, and would not give up the idea. He clasped his hands together and faced the ten directions and worshiped, saying, "Buddhas and Bodhisattvas of the ten directions, have pity on me and allow me to fulfill my vow today," then he had himself tied to a tree and said, "Now, take my head and present it." The fortuneteller drew his sword and advanced. At that time the deity of the tree struck the fortuneteller in the head with his hand, and the fortuneteller fell to the earth.

The king then said to the deity of the tree, "If you do not allow me to fulfill my vow you will be standing in the way of good works."

At this the deity no longer interfered. Thus, the fortuneteller cut off the king's head, and all of the people, from the queens and the imperial princes to the ministers and the bureaucrats and the common people, wept and their grief was boundless. The fortuneteller took the king's head back to the neighboring country.

Now this king, Daikō Myōō, was none other than the present Shakamuni Buddha. It is said that the neighboring king who hired the fortuneteller was the present Diabakuta.

As a quick footnote to the tale, it should be mentioned that Daibakuta was an enemy of the historical Buddha, a person who was well versed in religious matters and in scholarship but who was never able to best Buddha in debate. Some other versions of the story hold that this character was represented not by the neighboring king, but by the fortuneteller who was sent to collect the head of the hero.[2]

In any event, it is easy to appreciate the ideal of self-sacrifice that is stressed in this tale, even if the sacrifice does not seem to help anyone but the hero of the story. This story is typical of the tales found in the didactic section of the Indian stories, and not only because of the element of self sacrifice; it also provides an example of the *Jātaka*-like tales which the *Konjaku* compiler apparently took great delight in.

The *Jātaka* is a collection of tales of the previous incarnations of Buddha and his main disciples, and several stories from this collection can be found in *Konjaku Monogatari-shū*. The typical format for such stories is the same as the tale translated above. Buddha would relate some story of a noble deed to his disciples, then explain that the characters in the story were himself and various disciples in some previous existence. The stories are not used to explain specific events, but are intended to demonstrate virtuous actions and to dramatize the idea of rebirth in various existences.

In order to understand this point more fully, it will be helpful to compare the story above to another of the Indian tales, III. 14. This is a tale of the ugly daughter of a king whose wife is renowned for her beauty. The parents are ashamed of their daughter's looks and conceal her from the world, but when they begin receiving marriage proposals they quickly arrange for her marriage to one of the king's ministers in order to keep the secret within the family. When Buddha then appears at the palace for a sutra dedication the ugly daughter wishes to attend; suddenly her looks are changed and she becomes beautiful.

Buddha explains the transformation by saying that the daughter had served in a previous existence as a kitchen helper to the father, who once ordered the entire household to make offerings to a monk. Although the daughter/servant girl complied with the order, she derided the monk because he was ugly. Consequently, she was reborn as the ugly daughter of her former master. When she expressed the desire to honor Buddha, however, her looks were transformed and she no longer brought dishonor on her father.

Both the tale of the ugly daughter and that of the benevolent king are based on the idea of transmigration, or the cycle of birth and rebirth, and show that men's fates in their present existences are to some degree determined by their actions in previous existences. The thrust of the two tales, however, is considerably different.

The story of the ugly daughter is a tale of praise, dealing specifically with the *samgha,* or community of monks. The main point of the tale is to show the power of Buddhism, and this it does by demonstrating both the punishment one might incur by mistreating a monk and the superior knowledge of Buddha himself, who is able to explain the present by looking back to the past. It is not a story which urges any particular code of conduct on its readers, but rather is one calculated to impress them by revealing truth. The didactic tale, however, was intended to dramatize a virtue—self-sacrifice—rather than power. Both tales contain a sense of immediacy and proximity to the original action, which characterizes the Indian stories in general. Because the stories are dealing with a time when Buddha was either still in the world or had just passed out of it, they convey a sense of freshness that one will not find in either the Chinese or the Japanese tales.

There is a total of 185 stories extant in these first five volumes, and the general organization of their content is as follows:

Volume I—Thirty-six extant tales, two missing. They deal with the life of the historical Buddha from the time of his conception as a human and go through his religious searchings to his eventual enlightenment.

Volume II—Forty-one tales. They cover mostly the various sermons of Buddha in which he explicated the Buddhist law by interpreting various events in terms of the laws of cause and effect.

Volume III—Thirty-five tales. They recount various miracles associated with Buddha after his enlightenment and describe both his death and the deaths of his father and mother.

Volume IV—Forty-one tales. They deal with the works of Buddha's disciples after their master's death.

Volume V—Thirty-two tales. These are mostly concerned with previous lives of people and the effects these existences have had on the present. As mentioned, many are about the previous lives of Buddha himself and some are associated with the *Jātaka*. Many of these tales are animal stories.

Such is the content of the individual volumes. According to Kunisaki's grouping, the Indian tales are arranged as follows:

History:	I.1–I.8	
Praise:	a.	Buddha—I.9–I.38.
	b.	The Law—Volume II.
	c.	*Samgha* (monks)—Volumes III and IV
Didacticism:	Volume V.	

In these opening volumes the compiler has given us the background needed to understand what Buddhism is and how it works in its purest form. This background having been established, the

compiler then moves his focus to China, and the workings of
Buddhism in that country. Let us see how he handles this
material.

The Chinese Stories

There are 181 stories extant in volumes VI to X of *Konjaku
Monogatari-shū;* this total, it will be remembered, is for four
rather than five volumes, because volume VIII is missing. When
we remember that the five Indian volumes contained one hundred
and eighty-five stories, we can see that the compiler has picked
up his tempo as he has gotten closer to Japan. In addition to the
Buddhist stories, the China volumes also contain secular stories,
something we did not see in the first five volumes.

The content of the four extant volumes and the one missing
volume is as follows:

Volume VI—Forty-eight tales. Begins with the spread of
Buddhism through China, and moves to stories in praise of both
the Buddha and the Law.

Volume VII—Forty-seven extant stories, one missing. Stories
in praise of the Law, mostly the Lotus Sutra.

Volume VIII—Although this entire volume is missing in all
manuscripts, it is likely that it contained stories in praise of the
Bodhisattvas.

Volume IX—Forty-six tales. These are generally didactic, including stories demonstrating the virtues of filial piety (tales
1–12), and stories about cause and effect. Many are set in the
netherworld, and deal with the adventures of people who have
died and returned to life.

Volume X—Forty tales. Labeled "secular" by the compiler,
they recount well-known incidents from Chinese history and episodes about famous figures in Chinese religions, such as Confucius, Lao-Tzu, and Chuang Tzu.

Kunisaki's classification of the Chinese Buddhist tales is as
follows:

History: VI. 1–10.
             a.   Buddha—VI. 11–30.

> b. Law—VI.31–VIII.49.
> c. *Samgha*—VIII(?).
> Didacticism: Volume IV.

There seems no reason to doubt Kunisaki's speculations that the stories in volume VIII were intended to deal with praise of monks; it is likely that many of them would have been in praise of Kannon (Chinese Kuan Yin), the Bodhisattva of Mercy, who was extremely popular in both China and Japan.

As an example of the general tone of the Chinese tales, let us consider the following story, VI.11, "How the T'ang Dynasty Chinese An-liang of Wu Was Brought Back to Life by a Statue of Buddha Made by His Brother."

Long ago, in China during the T'ang dynasty, there was a person called An-liang of Wu in a county called Han in the state of Yu. His courtesy name was Tzu. This person for many years made a living by the taking of life, and the amount of killing that he had done over the years was so staggering as to be uncountable. Also, he never did any good works.

Now when An-liang was thirty-seven years old he went to the mountains to hunt, and just as he was about to shoot a large deer he unexpectedly fell from his horse, collapsed on the ground, and suddenly died. His retainers all gathered around him and grieved, and after half a day had passed he came back to life. An-liang sat up, wept bitterly, flung his body to the ground, and prayed for forgiveness.

His retainers asked him what had happened, but he was weeping and said nothing. After a while he told them this story:

"When I fell from my horse and collapsed on the ground all of a sudden demons with horses' and cows' heads appeared, with a large cart. Just as I was wondering, 'What kind of cart could this be?' they grabbed my body and tossed it into the cart. There were raging flames in the cart burning my body, and the heat was difficult to endure.

"Then they took me to King Yama, but suddenly a holy monk appeared—I didn't know who it was. When King Yama saw this monk he came right down from his throne, clasped his hands and worshiped the monk, saying to him, 'Why have you honored us with your presence, sir?'

"The monk said in reply, 'This sinner is one of my followers. I have come here to ask for a bit more life for him.' King Yama said, 'This is an extremely sinful person, and it would normally be difficult to release him, but because it's you, I'll hand him over. I don't regret it.' And so saying, he released me.

"At that time the monk took me away. Within my joyous heart there was also some doubt, and so I asked the monk, 'Who is it that has saved my life?'

"The monk replied, 'Don't you know me? I am the Buddha that your older brother An-tao had made because of his religious heart. You were his younger brother and you gave him thirty pieces of cash to help him have the image made. Because you gave him a little money even though you had no faith he was able to have the image made, and so I have come here to save you. Take a good look at my clothing.'

"Then he disappeared and I was reborn. Therefore, I threw my body to the ground and prayed for forgiveness for the sin of all the lives I have taken over the years."

After that he went to the home of his older brother An-tao and looked at the image of Buddha there; its clothing did not differ at all from that he had seen in the world of the dead. When An-liang saw this he shed even more tears and went home, and his own faith welled up from within him. He made an image of Buddha and worshiped and revered it.

When we think about this we see that even though he did not make this image of Buddha himself, there is uncountable virtue in giving even a speck of dust toward helping someone else make an image. It is said that Buddha considers this assistance to be the same type of virtue as making the image.

Having spent the first five volumes of his collection showing self-sacrifice and the actual power of the historical Buddha, in the Chinese tales the compiler of necessity begins to change his emphasis. This story, as is the case with many of the Chinese tales, focuses on the power of the image of Buddha, rather than on the man himself. We may conclude that Buddha is still important to the compiler, but that it is now a different experience, with the faithful forced to rely on images rather than the real thing.

In addition to this, the sutras come in for a considerable amount of praise in the Chinese section, with sixty-six stories devoted to this topic. Clearly and naturally, the world had entered a time when it was necessary to look to the symbols of Buddhism for help in attaining enlightenment, and not unnaturally the tales reflect this reality. Rather than demonstrating the wisdom of Buddha and his disciples, the compiler is now interested in showing the power of the symbols, for it is this power that will help his readers succeed in the world.

Accordingly, he portrays mostly the rewards for the faithful and the horrible punishments awaiting those who have sinned, often combining these two motifs as he did in the story translated above, showing how even an apparently inconsequential act of merit might serve to rescue a person from the fires of hell. Simply put, the emphasis has been moved from the source of the power to the affect of the power on mortals, or sometimes even others.

That the power of Buddhism was far-reaching can be seen in VII.21, in which a holy monk who recites the Lotus Sutra is approached one day on his way to the lavatory by a demon who asks him to have that sutra copied so that the demon might escape his unhappy incarnation. The demon gives the monk directions to a place where he had hidden a good deal of money in his previous lifetime, and the monk uses this money to have the sutra copied. The demon then reports to the monk in a dream that, thanks to the power of the sutra, he is no longer fated to a life of eating the excrement he finds in latrines, but he has been reborn in a new life. This story ends with a short moral extolling the power of the Lotus Sutra.

The tales of history in the Chinese Buddhist volumes are generally—and, for the most part, rightfully—considered by Japanese scholars to have less literary value than the other tales in these volumes. This is because these stories are often nearly word-for-word translations of written Chinese sources and frequently lack narrative interest. A major exception to this general rule, and a story which is worth spending some time considering, is VI.6, which deals with several adventures of a famous Chinese monk who went to India to collect sutras.

The monk in question is Hsüan Tsang (c. 596–664), who was the founder of the so-called "Mere ideation" school of Buddhism, the first of the Chinese sects to incorporate the teachings of Mahayana Buddhism. Among the most important of these teachings, incidentally, is the dominant position given the bodhisattva and other figures which have the power to help bring mortals to enlightenment.

Hsüan Tsang, in any event, is himself a folk hero in China and Japan, and is the principal hero of the sixteenth-century novel *Hsi Yü Chi,* or "Journey to the West" (translated into English by Arthur Waley under the title *Monkey).*[3] Although none of the episodes in the *Konjaku* tale occurs in the novel and the character of the hero is handled rather differently in the two works, the *Konjaku* story is important because it demonstrates that stories about Hsüan Tsang were circulating by at least the late eleventh century, or about three hundred years before the novel was written.

There are various written sources for most of the episodes in the *Konjaku* tale, but the compiler has woven several different stories from different sources into one unified whole here. There is at least one part of the story for which we have no known written source.[4]

In the *Konjaku* tale we first see Hsüan Tsang on his travels in an area apparently deserted by people. He notices lights, and wondering if there are people in the vicinity, goes toward them, but the lights are being held by demons and not by people. The monk recites the Heart Sutra and the demons flee.

The next episode relates how Hsüan Tsang learned this sutra. According to the tale, he was traveling in the mountains when he came across an apparently dead person from whom a terrible odor emanated; this person turned out to be a yet-alive woman afflicted with a disease which had covered her with boils. She informed the monk that she had been told that if someone were to suck the discharge from her boils she would be cured. The compassionate monk was moved by this story and overcame his revulsion to do as asked. The woman then revealed herself to be Kannon (Chinese Kuan Yin), the Bodhisattva of Mercy, and as a reward for his compassion presented him with the Heart Sutra.

After this digression the narrative once more joins the monk on his travels and describes how he meets an Indian teacher who has been informed of his arrival in a dream and has been saved from death specifically to teach the Chinese monk. Hsüan Tsang learns the new doctrines quickly and pushes on to visit the holy places in India, but his boat is captured by pirates.

The pirates decide to sacrifice him to their own deity because he is so handsome, but are converted to Buddhism by a miracle which takes place just as they are about to kill him. Hsüan Tsang then receives the sutras he is to take back to China but is stopped from crossing a river by a dragon who desires a magic begging bowl he has been presented. Hsüan Tsang gives the dragon the bowl and goes on his way.

In the later novel the hero is depicted as a weak character while on his pilgrimage to India, one constantly in need of rescue by his chief disciple. This disciple is a stone monkey king on his own search for enlightenment. The weakness of Hsüan Tsang is a source of a good deal of humor in the novel, but this humor is missing completely from the *Konjaku* tale, where the compassion of the monk and the power he has achieved from this compassion are the chief ingredients.

There are, however, some points of comparison between the *Konjaku* tale and *Monkey*. In both Hsüan Tsang is associated with the Bodhisattva of Mercy and with the Heart Sutra; in addition, the episode in *Konjaku* in which Hsüan Tsang must give the dragon his begging bowl before being allowed to cross the river is similar to an incident in the novel in which the characters must bribe the keeper of the Buddha's storehouse before they are presented with the sutras they have come to collect. In both episodes the monk must part with a valuable begging bowl.

There is no trace of the monkey in the *Konjaku,* though he is the real hero of the novel.

It seems likely that Hsüan Tsang was a true folk hero in Japan, and that many tales about him would have been familiar to the audience of the collection. This tale is well told, with vivid descriptions, and retains most of the excitement and immediacy that a work taken from oral circulation might be expected to have contained.

Especially significant about this story is that it depicts a person who is as close in his actions to Buddha as it is possible to become. He is self-sacrificing, compassionate, and wise, and his "reward" is the power he receives from the sutras and the bodhisattvas.

Self-denial is one of the two major themes in the didactic tales contained in volume IX. These stories are broken into two major parts, one group stressing the virtue of filial piety and the other treating the motif of death, redemption, and rebirth. The idea of filial piety is, of course, associated with Confucian thought, but it was important to the *Konjaku* compiler, who includes stories about it in both his Chinese and Japanese sections. If we remember that *Konjaku Monogatari-shū* was produced during a period of social instability and chaos it is perhaps not difficult to understand the compiler's concern with family relations and domestic order, but there is another reason, I believe, for his use of stories about filial piety within the Buddhist sections of the collection.

The compiler seems to have thought that it was mostly through family relationships that a person could hope to emulate the most important of the virtues of Buddha, that of self-denial, and this, I believe, is the main reason he includes stories which are more properly secular in his Buddhist sections. The Chinese tales describe the various types of sacrifices children can make for their parents, and one tale (IX.7) even relates the story of a youth who throws his own body into the bay where his father drowned because he fears that he will otherwise never see his father's body and not to pay respect to it would be unfilial.

Konjaku Monogatari-shū, it will be remembered, is a Buddhist work, but the compiler is concerned basically with helping his readers get by in a difficult world. When within the family one demonstrates the virtues of Buddha, then, this is something to be lauded, and it is moreover something which will eventually help the individual involved because it will result in his accumulating more merit, which will help him escape various punishments in the world to come.

An interesting reversal on the theme of the duties of children to their parents is found in IX.17, in which a mother who has withheld rice from her son for her own consumption is returned to the household after her death in the form of a horse. Unaware that the horse is the reincarnation of his mother, the son frequently abuses it when it will not perform the excessive tasks he has required of it. Son and daughter are informed of the truth in a dream and the mother is finally saved by their religious acts.

This tale is significant both because it shows what is in store for those who are not aware of the importance of self-sacrifice, and also because it shows the willingness of the children to forgive their mother and work for her redemption. It combines the motif of filial piety with that of retribution, thereby combining the two most important motifs in the Chinese Buddhist section, and in particular in the didactic stories. It demonstrates that the idea of filial piety is not merely an abstract rule of conduct, but is important for success in avoiding punishments awaiting those who are misled by any of the tempting false doctrines alive in this age of *zōbō*.

Stories 13 to 46 of volume IX are about retribution for evil acts and depict people reborn as animals, the punishment of those who have taken life, and the punishments meted out in the nether world to those who have behaved badly in the world of the living. Some of them also feature heroes who are able to escape punishments for sins by repenting and doing good works, but more often than not those who sin receive their just deserts.

In the Chinese volumes we find, for the first time, stories which are secular. These are contained in volume X, and might be said to offer a short course in what the Japanese of the eleventh and twelfth centuries considered the highlights of Chinese history and wisdom. They follow their written sources much less faithfully than do the Chinese Buddhist tales, and it is likely that most of them were in oral circulation in Japan, if only in a narrow circle of educated people.

These stories begin with a general history of China up to the time of the compilation of *Konjaku* and go on to include several tales about famous people from Chinese history. Perhaps one of the most interesting of these is the *Konjaku* version of the story of the rebellion of An Lu Shan and the death of the concubine of Emperor Hsüan Tsung, the notorious beauty Yang Kuei-fei, X.7. This story was extremely popular among the Japanese aristocracy, having enough romance and tragedy to seize the Heian imagination; part of the reason for the popularity was the long poem by Po Chü-yi, "The Song of Everlasting Sorrow."[5]

In brief, the story tells about the emperor's all-consuming love for the woman and how this love eventually leads to a rebellion by the general An Lu Shan. When the emperor is forced to flee the city his followers insist on putting the woman to death.

According to the *Konjaku* story—and the poem—the emperor commissioned a Taoist adept to travel to the land of the dead and talk with his lover after the rebellion was quashed and he was restored to his throne. The adept did so, and returned bearing pledges of her undying love.

Although the plot of the *Konjaku* tale appears to have been taken from Po's poem, the text of the story cannot be traced to any written source. The *Konjaku* compiler is more interested in the pathos of the situation than in the recording of history, though, and it is more likely that his knowledge of the tale came from information which would have been "common knowledge" among the Japanese aristocracy.

This is probably the case with many of the Chinese history tales, for these tales depict events with which the average aristocratic Japanese would have been familiar. They are not history so much as they are capsule summaries of the events every educated person should have some knowledge of; they might be called the Heian version of a College Outline Series course on Chinese history.

Others of the Chinese secular tales are about famous people. A good example is X.9, which describes how the famous philosopher Confucius is made a fool of by a young boy he meets on the road, and X.13, which praises the wisdom of the Taoist philosopher Chuang Tzu. A part of this latter has no known written source; either the source is no longer extant or the story was taken from oral tradition. A thorough study of these Chinese historical stories should reveal much about the Japanese knowledge of and attitudes toward Chinese history in the Heian period.

All in all, the secular Chinese stories have been placed in the collection for educational purposes, and the Japanese doubtless read them for what they could learn from them. They provide us with an excellent avenue through which we can arrive at a more complete understanding of the influence Chinese culture had in Heian Japan.

In summary, the Chinese tales contained in volumes VI to X bring us from the historical Buddha and the events surrounding the rise of Buddhism in India to a glorification of the power of the image of Buddha and the various sutras which have been associated with the religion. The emphasis gradually shifts from the virtues of self-denial to the horrible things which can happen in the next life to people who have not followed Buddhist law. The theme of self-denial, so important in the Indian stories, is most common here in the context of filial piety, which is perhaps the major area where man can duplicate the behavior of Buddha. In addition to the Buddhist tales, volume X of the collection offers a short course in Chinese history and culture. Now let us examine the stories in the Japanese Buddhist section of the collection.

The Japanese Buddhist Stories

There are ten volumes of Buddhist stories set in Japan, one of which—volume XVIII—is no longer extant. A brief summary of their subject matter follows:

Volume XI—Thirty-three extant tales, five missing. Deals with the early history of Buddhism in Japan, from its introduction to founding of the important temples.

Volume XII—Forty tales. The history tales continue, with stories about the most important Buddhist festivals. Also contains stories of praise, both for Buddha and the law, in this case the Lotus Sutra.

Volume XIII—Forty-four stories. All in praise of the law, and all are about the Lotus Sutra.

Volume XIV—Forty-five stories. All in praise of the various sutras.

Volume XV—Fifty-four stories. These are all tales about people who have been reborn in the Western Paradise of Amida.

Volume XVI—Thirty-nine stories, one missing. These are tales in praise of monks, specifically the Bodhisattva Kannon, the Bodhisattva of Mercy.

Volume XVII—Fifty stories, all in praise of the various Bodhisattvas, the most popular being Jizō, known in Japan as the guardian of children.

Volume XVIII—No longer extant. It is likely that it, too, contained tales in praise of monks.

Volume XIX—Forty-one extant stories, three missing. All are didactic and they cover a wide range of subject matter. Best known are the first eighteen tales, which are about people who take the Buddhist vows.

Volume XX—Forty-four extant stories, two missing. All are didactic. The largest group of tales here concerns people who receive retribution for their sins in this life. A smaller group is about punishments one might receive in the world of the dead.

According to Kunisaki, the Japanese Buddhist tales are broken down as follows:

History:	XI. 1–XII. 10.	
Praise:	a.	Buddha: XII. 11–XII. 24.
	b.	Law: XII. 25–XV (inclusive).
	c.	Monks: XVI–XVIII(?)
Didacticism:	XIX and XX.	

There does not seem to be any reason to doubt Kunisaki's tentative assignment of the missing volume XVIII to the category of praise for monks.

Proportionally speaking the Japanese Buddhist section contains a much higher percentage of tales of history than does the Chinese section, a fact which should not be surprising. What is interesting, however, is that the Japanese Buddhist volumes contain such a higher percentage of tales about monks and the law than is to be found in the Chinese Buddhist volumes.

Roughly speaking, counting only the extant tales (and it should be remembered that there is one entire volume missing in the case of both the Chinese and Japanese Buddhist sections, and that in both cases the missing volume probably deals with stories in praise of monks), nearly 63 percent of the Japanese Buddhist tales are in praise of the law and monks, while in the case of the Chinese stories, the figure is 46 percent. On the other hand, about 14 percent of the Chinese Buddhist tales are in praise of the Buddha, while only slightly over 3 percent of the Japanese Buddhist tales are stories of this type.

These figures vividly demonstrate the great emphasis placed on sutras and Bodhisattvas by the Japanese Buddhists, and show also that the compiler of *Konjaku Monogatari-shū* tended to think of the Chinese as being closer to Buddha than he himself was. We have seen that the late Heian Japanese believed that they were living in an age that could not see the transmission of the true teachings of Buddha; the only way to attain salvation was to place one's faith in a powerful symbol, such as the Western Paradise of Amida or the Lotus Sutra, then hope for the best.

To give some idea of the flavor of such tales, I will present XII.37, "How the Monk Shinkei Was Able to Save His Parents from Death by the Power of the Lotus Sutra."

Long ago there was a man called the monk Shinkei. He was the child of the governor of Awa Province, the Duke Kanehiro. He was a disciple of the Tendai Risshi Kanmyō. From the time he was small he was a devotee of the Lotus Sutra and recited it day and night; also he studied esoteric Buddhism and practiced that day and night.

In time faith rose strongly in his heart and he abandoned all thoughts of worldly fame or profit, praying constantly for Buddhahood in the world to come. For this reason he left his mountain temple and went unexpectedly to Tanba province, where he secluded himself and recited the Lotus Sutra and practiced esoteric Buddhism, praying earnestly for enlightenment.

In time a young child of extraordinary appearance appeared before him. He did not know where this person had come from, and was rather suspicious, when the child faced him and recited in a most wondrous voice a poem asking the man to recite the Lotus Sutra. He listened to the monk recite the sutra for a time, then suddenly disappeared. The monk thought it strange and wondered where he had gone, and went looking for him, but the child was nowhere to be found. Finally, because he could not figure out who it was, he decided it must have been a child from heaven who had come to praise him, and he shed tears and thought its holiness boundless.

In time his father Kanehiro went to Awa Province to assume his post. Because his parents entreated him, the monk also went. In that province he had boundless influence, and the people of the province all bowed their heads and valued him without limit. At this the monk thought in his heart, "I have been reciting the Lotus Sutra for many years, and practicing the law, and must certainly have accumulated unfathomable merit. If one is in this world long, however, he begins to sin, and it is certain that he will remain in the cycle of birth and rebirth. So I wish to do none other than quickly die before I begin to sin."

He decided to take poison which would surely kill him, so first he tried one type, but he did not die. Then he heard of another which would definitely kill him, so he went to the mountains and gathered some, and took it secretly. Even so, he did not die, and thought, "This is a strange affair. Even though I've taken poison I do not die because of the power of the Lotus Sutra." And the lines "Neither sword nor staff shall harm him; poison shall not hurt him" came to his mind, and he thought it moving and sad without limit.

Then later in a dream a person came and told him, "You are a holy man and pure in your belief. Continue to recite the Lotus Sutra so well." When he looked closely at this man it was none other than the Bodhisattva Fugen. When he awoke his faith grew stronger and he continued to recite the sutra.

In time there was an epidemic and the monk was taken ill. His parents also became ill, and suffered from the disease. At this time he had another dream in which demons came and took him off to the underworld, where one of them said, "Release the monk, he is a devotee of the Lotus Sutra." And he was released. When he awoke, the monk grew well and his health was restored. His parents died, however.

When the monk saw them he wept, and still weeping recited the Lotus Sutra and prayed for their return to life. Again in a dream the monk saw the sixth volume of the Lotus Sutra fly down from the sky. There was a letter in the volume. He opened this and read, "Because you recited the Lotus Sutra and prayed for the rebirth of your parents their lives have already been extended and I am sending them back to you now. This is a letter from the King of the Underworld."

When he awoke and saw his parents, they had truly revived. The monk told them of his experiences with the Underworld. His parents, hearing about it, were happy and thought it boundlessly holy. All who heard about this shed tears and thought it holy.

This monk, during his lifetime, recited the Lotus Sutra a million times, and did other devotions day and night without rest.

The profit of the present world is like this—it is said that without doubt he was enlightened in the world to come.

This is an instructive story because it contains nearly all the elements stressed throughout the Japanese Buddhist tales. The hero Shinkei is a man who has devoted his life wholeheartedly to a single-minded religious purpose; further, he is filial and willing to use the powers he has accumulated in his religious devotions to assist his parents. Although he has supposedly abandoned all thoughts of the present life, he is clearly successful in this world. And the story stresses, as do many of the Japanese Buddhist tales, the power associated with holy things. In this case it is the Lotus Sutra, but the Bodhisattvas are treated in much the same way. Finally, the hero recognizes that he is weak by himself, and is willing to put his absolute trust in an external object. His miraculous powers and eventual salvation are the results of his devotion to the Lotus Sutra, and not wholly to his inherent Buddha-nature.

Many of these elements are already visible in the tales of history. These stories begin, naturally enough, with an account of the introduction of Buddhism to Japan by the Prince Regent Shōtoku, a story which was virtually obligatory. The fourth tale in volume XI begins a series in more or less chronological order of the stories of the men who introduced the various sects of Buddhism to Japan, but the second and third tales in this volume are of some note because they are about two men who do not appear in any sort of official Buddhist hierarchy.

These men are the lay monk Gyōki (670–749),[6] and the supposed founder of a school of ascetic religious training known as Shugendō, a man known as En no Ubasoku.[7] It is significant that the compiler has given these men the prominence in the collection that they have, for they both worked outside the Buddhist hierarchy and were both moved by a strong religious conviction. Each dedicated his entire life to a single-minded religious devotion, which is apparently what impressed the *Konjaku* compiler.

Gyōki was a preacher who converted the masses and did good works for public welfare; because his efforts tended to remove people from the tax roles he was eventually punished by the government. He was popular with the people, who called him a Bodhisattva. According to *Konjaku*, he "had a heart which was deeply compassionate, and he felt pity for the people just as the Buddha had."

The story of his clash with the established authorities is reported symbolically in XI.2 through the tale of his disagreements with a scholar-monk called Wakō. According to this story, Wakō belittled Gyōki's achievements as a Buddhist, but then he died, and was given the message that Gyōki was a great man, and was sent back to life to inform others of this truth. The clash here is between a type of scholarly Buddhism which had been prevalent in Japan until that time, and the more active, evangelical Buddhism advocated by Gyōki and his followers. The compiler's treatment of Gyōki leaves no question as to where his own sympathies were.

Because of his help in raising money for the building of the Tōdai-ji temple, Gyōki was eventually rehabilitated by the Buddhists and thus enjoyed some official blessing, but it is nonetheless significant that the compiler has chosen this type of person to be placed second to the Prince Regent Shōtoku.

En no Ubasoku had in some ways the opposite type of character from Gyōki, for he was a hermit who had very little public visibility, while Gyōki was an active preacher. Nonetheless, both men had devotion and powers which their devotion had helped them to attain, and it is clear that this is what impressed the *Konjaku* compiler.

The other tales in the history section are about the founding of the major temples and sects in Japan, the establishment of the important festivals and the like.

The stories of praise in the Japanese Buddhist section total nearly seven volumes if we count the missing volume XVIII among them. As I noted above, the vast majority of these tales are about monks and the law rather than the Buddha.

The most important single sutra praised in these tales is the Lotus Sutra; some eighty-nine tales (XII.24–XIV.29) are about the power of this sutra and the miracles associated with it. As for monks, the most important are the Bodhisattvas Kannon (Bodhisattva of Mercy) and Jizō (known as the guardian of children). All three of these figures should be thought of as mediators, objects which had the power to bring mortals closer to the Buddha. The fact that such a small percentage of the Buddhist tales concern the Buddha himself, or his images, is indicative of the fact that the Heian Buddhists did not see direct communication as being possible.

The Lotus Sutra was the most important scripture of the Tendai sect, which, as we have seen, was probably the home sect of the *Konjaku* compiler. In addition to this sutra, incidentally, Tendai followers held Amida and his Pure Land in great reverence; volume XV consists entirely of stories about people reborn in this paradise. Generally speaking, the Lotus Sutra was believed to profit people in this world, by saving them from danger as the hero of the story translated above was saved. The Pure Land, of course, was considered as salvation for the life to come.

As is evident from the story quoted above, sincerity and devoutness of heart were absolutely essential to the person who practiced devotions to the Lotus Sutra and to those who believed in the Pure Land. The compiler informs us at the end of XII.29, for example:

Thus, it is said that even though one might make images of the Buddha or copy sutras, this is not enough; one should work with a thoroughly devout heart.

In the case of the Lotus Sutra this referred to one's frame of mind when copying or chanting the sutra, and in the case of Pure Land belief to the recitation of the name of Amida.

Stories about those who were reborn in Amida's Western Paradise generally follow a standard formula. The hero is introduced, frequently with some evidence which shows he was destined for great things from the beginning; his religious credentials, including the name of his teacher and the types of devotions he practiced if those are known, are established; any miracles associated with him during his lifetime are reported; and the circumstances of his successful rebirth are reported. This formula is identical to that found in the *Ōjō den,*[8] although the *Konjaku* compiler typically embellishes his tales.

Amida, or Amitaba, is a Buddha who vowed to postpone his own enlightenment until all living creatures were saved. The Western Paradise over which he presides is a sort of halfway house from which those who have placed their trust in him can be reborn and in which they will be able to live the life necessary to attain final enlightenment. Belief in the possibility of rebirth in this paradise was a key factor in Heian Buddhism, and by the middle of the Kamakura period two new sects had been founded based purely on the idea of the Western Paradise.

Those who aspired to such rebirth chanted the name of Amida using the formula "Namu Amida Butsu," or "I rely on thee,

Amida." There are records of people making this chant thousands of times daily.

While in *Konjaku* devotion to the Lotus Sutra or to Amida generally entails a long period of religious practice, this is usually not the case in Bodhisattva worship. Sincerity is, of course, important in these tales, but what is generally stressed first is the compassion of the Bodhisattva. It is often the case that a person who is in some sort of trouble will make a spontaneous, sincere plea to a Bodhisattva even though he or she may not have been a longtime devotee to the Bodhisattva; in such cases help is generally forthcoming.

For example, XVI.8 tells of a poor woman who prays to the Kannon and is given money; there are many such tales. In XVI.19 a Korean queen is punished for adultery by her husband by being tied to a tree by her hair, suspended several feet above the ground. She prays to a Japanese Kannon and is given a golden platform for support, which is invisible to all but the queen.

The Kannon was also known to appear miraculously to save people from being wounded by arrows. In this cycle of tales the hero finds that the statue of Kannon which he worships has been mysteriously pierced by an arrow.

Another popular Bodhisattva is Jizō, the hero of the first thirty-two tales in volume XVII. He is a particularly Japanese deity who had special powers over children and exercised a good deal of influence in the underworld. Many of the tales concerning him tell how he has saved people from death for some kindness they have done in the world of the living.[9]

To reiterate, the Lotus Sutra and, to a lesser degree, the Pure Land, entailed long-term religious devotion and sincerity of heart, but the Bodhisattva was more a spur-of-the-moment type of savior. This is not to say, of course, there was no long-term worship of Bodhisattvas, or that there was no spontaneous appeal to the Lotus Sutra or Amida, but only that these are the tendencies found in *Konjaku*. Nearly all of the stories in the volumes of praise stress the idea that man by himself is almost helpless and that he must therefore put his faith in one or another of the holy, powerful Buddhist symbols such as sutras or Bodhisattvas.

The didactic tales in volumes XIX and XX cover a wide range of subject matter but stress above all the workings of the law of cause and effect. Some of the subjects covered are the taking of Buddhist vows, filial piety, the misuse of Buddhist property, encounters with various types of superhuman beings, and the experiences of people in the land of the dead. Many of these tales appear to have been taken directly from oral tradition. One has the impression that the compiler is attempting to explain unusual events by the use of Buddhist principles.

One of the most interesting of the Japanese didactic tales is XIX.15, which is the story of a violent man who has no knowledge of or sympathy toward Buddhism. One day he passes a temple and on impulse storms into it during a service. He demands to know what Buddhism is all about and the frightened speaker tells him that there is a Buddha in the West named Amida who will have mercy on any who entreat him, but prefers those who have taken the Buddhist vows much as a father prefers his own children.

The hero cuts his own hair off on the spot and vows to continue traveling West until Amida answers his calls. Finally he is answered by a voice from the sea which responds to his question, "Hey, there, Amida, where are you?" with the words, "I'm in here." The hero soon dies, leaving signs that prove that he has been reborn in the Western Paradise. This type of dramatic and sincere dedication to a single purpose is, as we have seen, among the things admired most by the compiler.

Other didactic tales depict retribution for various sins. Chief among these sins is the misuse of Buddhist property. In XIX.19 a monk lost in the mountains happens across the site for punishing dead monks who are guilty of this sin. The living monk watches in terror as the dead monks (who have the same physical sensations as the living) are crucified and have molten copper poured through their mouth until it comes out of their nose, ears, eyes and such. He realizes that this is a warning to him and vows never again to misuse Buddist temple property.[10]

Some of the didactic tales seem to have but tenuous ties to Buddhism. In XX.10, for example, we have an entertaining story about a man who attempts to learn the art of making penises disappear. He is unsuccessful, but is able to learn to make shoes and other small objects fly. The didactic message of this story is somewhat weak—we are told that the practice of such arts is a sin and should be avoided.

In summary, the Japanese Buddhist tales contained in volumes XI through XX stress above all the necessity to devote oneself wholeheartedly to some powerful Buddhist symbol in order to attain salvation. The stories provide a comprehensive view of Buddhism from its beginnings to its present state in Japan, but more importantly, they provide a model for the contemporary audience to follow in order to lead a religious life. What role, then, do the secular tales play in the collection?

The Japanese Secular Tales

Volumes XXI (which is no longer extant) through XXXI of *Konjaku Monogatari-shū* are "secular" rather than "Buddhist." They include a variety of stories drawn from as large a variety of sources and are considered by most readers to be the most rewarding tales in the collection. One scholar has even gone so far as to suggest that the compiler was essentially bored in his gathering of the first twenty volumes, ploughing on only so that he could arrive at these last two hundred and ninety-nine tales (seventeen of these are no longer extant, leaving a total of two hundred eighty-two) which were the real rationale for his work.[11]

Given the vast amount of planning that we have seen in the first volumes, it is difficult to imagine that anyone but the most dedicated masochist would subject himself to such tortures, but it remains true that scholars have seen the secular tales as a breed apart. The following is a brief summary of the volumes and their contents:

Volume XXI—No longer extant. Thought to have contained stories about the Japanese Imperial Family.

Volume XXII—Eight stories. They deal with the powerful families in Japanese history, especially the Fujiwara family.

Volume XXIII—Fourteen tales, with another twelve missing. About the exploits of strong people, including some women.

Volume XXIV—Fifty-five stories, two others missing. About people who have excelled in the arts.

Volume XXV—Twelve stories, two others missing. This is one of the most famous of the volumes in the collection because all its tales are about warriors and battles, which were to become the subjects of a good deal of subsequent Japanese literature.

Volume XXVI—Twenty-three stories. All deal with the workings of karma.

Volume XXVII—Thirty-five stories. About spirits, good and bad.

Volume XXVIII—Forty-four stories. All are tales of humor.

Volume XXIX—Forty stories. They are about evil actions and the retribution for evil.

Volume XXX—Fourteen stories. Primarily these are about relationships between men and women; they contain a large number of poems.

Volume XXXI—Thirty-seven stories. Labeled "miscellaneous," they deal with various miraculous and unusual events.

Kunisaki's division of the stories into groups of history, praise, and didacticism, which we have observed in the Buddhist sections of the collection, can also be applied, with some modifications, to the secular tales. A further level of organization is present here as well—about half of the volumes contain stories set in the capital, while the others contain stories set in the provinces. By and large, these alternate. The following is Kunisaki's organization:

History: This, it is postulated, would be the tales in volume XXI, which is no longer extant.

Praise: There are two categories in this division, rather than the three in the Buddhist volumes. These are stories in praise of power and stories in praise of proficiency in some way of life. The stories praising power are in volume XXII (set in the capital) and volume XXIII (set in the provinces), and those in praise of proficiency are in volume XXIV (capital) and volume XXV (provinces).

Didacticism: These include the remainder of the volumes. Kunisaki breaks them down into three types: tales of the unusual, tales which are entertaining, and legends. Each of these three subcategories is composed of two volumes, and one of the two in each case is centered in the capital, with the other centered in the provinces. The exact organization is as follows:

Tales of the unusual: volume XXVI (provinces) and volume XXVII (capital).

Entertaining tales: volume XXVIII (capital) and volume XXIX (provinces).

Legends: volume XXX (capital) and volume XXXI (provinces).

Although these secular tales are generally seen as a breed apart, as I have noted, there are some similarities between them and the Buddhist tales which should be noted. Primary among these is the importance placed on dedication to a particular way of life, which is a motif running through many of the secular stories. In addition to this, the compiler seems to be using the secular stories in much the same way he used the Buddhist ones—to teach his audience how to get along better in a troubled world. Sincerity, dedication, and a quick wit are the attributes which are most important to success in the world.

To illustrate this, let us consider the following tale, XXIV.5, "How Kudara no Kawanari and the Craftsman Hida Competed."

Long ago there was an artist called Kudara no Kawanari. He was a man unparalleled in this world. He created the statue of the dragon at the Waterfall Pavillion, and he is also the man who did the painting on the wall of this temple.

Once a youth he had employed ran away. He searched in the East and the West but could not find him, so he hired a servant from a certain powerful family and said to him, "A servant boy I have employed for some time has run away. I want you to go find him and bring him back." The servant said, "That's easy enough—if I just knew what he looked like I could catch him. If I don't know what he looks like, how can I catch him?"

Kawanari said, "That's true," and he took out some paper and drew a likeness of the servant boy and handed it to the servant, saying, "Just grab any boy that looks like this. The East and West markets are places where many people gather; you're bound to find him in one of them."

The servant took the drawing of the boy's face and went to the market. There were many people there, but none who resembled the servant boy. Just when he was wondering if he should stay any longer there appeared a youth who matched the drawing. He took out the drawing and compared it to the youth; there was not the slightest difference. Thinking, "This is the one," he captured the youth and took him back to Kawanari.

Kawanari was extremely happy when he saw he had his servant boy back. All who heard about this thought it was a remarkable event.

Now at about this time there was a craftsman called the craftsman of Hida. He did much of the work when the capital was moved, and he was a craftsman without parallel in the world. Buraku Hall was his work; it is certainly a wonderful place.

Now this craftsman often competed in various things with this Kawanari. The craftsman of Hida said to Kawanari, "I have built a small hall on my grounds and would like for you to look at it. I've been thinking I'd like to get you to do some artwork on my walls."

"Even though we're competing its always been in fun—that's why he's talking like this," thought Kawanari, and he went to the craftsman of Hida's house. When he got there he saw a truly unusual-looking little hall, with doors in all four walls, all opened.

The craftsman of Hida said, "Go on in the hall and look around," so Kawanari went up on the veranda and started in by the south door. The door suddenly slammed shut, however. He was surprised, and went around to the west door, but that door too slammed shut, and the south door opened again. So he went to the north door, but that door shut, and the west door opened. Then he went to the east door, but that door shut and the north door opened. He went around the building like this countless times but he could not figure out the openings and closings and finally left the veranda in a huff. The laughter of the craftsman of Hida was boundless. Kawanari was angry, and went on home.

Several days later Kawanari sent word to the craftsman of Hida: "Please come to my house. There's something there I want to show you."

The craftsman thought, "He's surely trying to trick me," and did not go, but Kawanari asked him most politely several times, so the craftsman went to Kawanari's house eventually. His arrival was announced and the artist sent word, "Come in here."

Following these instructions he went down a hall and through a door, where he saw a large person swollen up and black, lying dead, and the odor filled his nose. He had not expected to find anything like this, and, frightened, let out a yell, and ran out of the room.

Kawanari was inside and when he heard the yell his laughter was boundless. The craftsman of Hida was frightened, and planted his feet on the ground, when from behind the door came the face of Kawanari, who said, "Hey, you, I'm in here—come on in."

Frightened, he approached and looked—there on the paper door, by damn, was painted a picture of a dead man. The artist had done it out of revenge for having been tricked at the hall.

All these two did were like this. It is said that this tale was widely repeated at the time and was praised by all.

This tale is truly a celebration of the talents of its two heroes, and as such is representative of many of the stories in the *Konjaku* secular volumes. The compiler admired proficiency in nearly any field, and he seemed to feel that dedication to some way of life and obtaining proficiency in it was essential to any kind of earthly success. While he clearly preferred a Buddhist way of life, it is obvious that he did not denigrate secular attainments. He does not seem ever to have lost sight of the fact that it is this world his readers were being forced to cope with.

From dedication and proficiency flow most of the rest of the motifs in the secular volumes. Stupidity, or lack of proficiency, is ridiculed by the compiler, and his sense of humor—as is evident from the tale quoted above—is also tied to these elements. The compiler admired quick wit, such as that shown by Kawanari in the above story, and he was also attracted to the unusual actions of his characters, who are themselves generally unusual.

There are, of course, other motifs in the secular volumes, but generally speaking the compiler intended to provide his readers with a blueprint for success in various fields of endeavor, and to do this he holds up successful models for praise and unsuccessful ones for ridicule.

Rather than go through the secular section volume by volume attempting to describe their contents, a task which would lengthen an already-long chapter, in the next few pages I shall summarize a few of the stories which praise success, ridicule failure, or which are tales of the unusual. This will give the reader some idea of the wide range of subject matter covered in the final eleven volumes of *Konjaku* while still demonstrating the basic unity of the collection.

The story related in XXIV.23 is instructive because it shows us what a person must go through in order to achieve proficiency in the cultured arts. In this tale, a prince who wishes to learn two obscure pieces on the lute goes secretly every night for three years to the hut of a blind musician, the only person who knows how to play them, in hopes of hearing them. Finally his patience is rewarded and the blind lute player teaches the prince the tunes. This dedication is highly praised by the compiler.

In volume XXV we have proficiency of a different kind, that in war and the martial arts. One of the most famous tales in this volume is XXV.12, in which a warrior and his son pursue and finally kill a horse thief. They leave their house separately and never speak to each other during the chase; they so thoroughly understand each other that one can always tell what the other is about to do. At the end of this tale the compiler comments that the hearts of warriors are strange things indeed. It seems he cannot help but admire their skill even though he has no basic sympathy for them as human beings.

The tales in volume XXX present another type of cleverness, this one the kind found in the more aristocratic court romances. The fourteen tales here all depict affairs between men and women. With the exception of the first story in the volume, they all contain poems. Some of the stories in this volume have parallel treatments in works such as *Yamato Monogatari,* which we know were widely read by Heian aristocratic audiences. Most stress the theme of *"aware,"* or that which is touching or moving to the reader, and contain poems, generally presented as proof of the heroes' good breeding and attainments.

Volume XXVIII contains tales of humor, though many of them are difficult for a modern audience—Western or Japanese, in some cases—to understand. Story 24 in this volume is interesting as a sort of transitional tale between cleverness and stupidity; in this tale a monk who claims to have stopped eating grain because of a religious vow is found out by a clever nobleman who looks through the monk's feces and discovers proof that he is lying in order to be rewarded for his supposed piety.

The nobleman in this case is praised for his quickness of wit, while the monk—who disappears in shame—is ridiculed for his stupidity.

Often, however, stupidity is not merely ridiculed, but is the source of some kind of disaster. In XXIX.39, for example, a woman who squats to urinate is seen by a snake and raped by it, an act which sends her into deep shock. The compiler intones, "Therefore, women who hear this story, you should never face a grove such as that one to do such things." The morals of the tales in volume XXIX tend to warn against acts which are not clever.

Shocking or unusual situations and the reactions of people to them are another source of interest to the *Konjaku* compiler. An example is XXIX.18, which relates how a man finds a woman stealing hair from corpses which have been stacked at the Rashōmon gate, a major entry into the city. The man is shocked but the old woman tells him that one must be resourceful to make it through the world in these difficult times, a lesson the man takes to heart by stealing the woman's clothes.

While the compiler was indeed interested in the reactions of people to such unusual situations, he was just as interested in the situations themselves on occasion. In XXVI.2 a man traveling a certain road through a certain province is suddenly overcome with sexual desire. Since there are no women available he enters a field, picks a turnip, cuts a hole in it and uses it to satisfy his desires. Then he discards it and goes on his way.

The following day the owner of the field arrives with his wife and daughters to harvest the crops. The youngest daughter finds the turnip with the hole in it and eats it. Soon she becomes pregnant, much to the astonishment of her family. She gives birth to a son, whom her family raises.

Later still, the man who had violated the turnip passes the spot once again, this time with friends. He remembers the place and tells his friends what transpired there the last time he passed by. The girl's mother overhears him, and drags him off to see the daughter and her baby; the baby of course resembles him in every detail. The man is moved by the strangeness of it all, decides the relationship must be fated by karma, and marries the mother of the baby. The compiler comments, "This is a very strange affair."

This story has clearly been told for its value as an unusual and entertaining story. There are no disastrous, or even potentially dangerous, consequences, although the man might be praised for his acceptance of his fate. Other tales about unusual situations, however, are not always so carefree.

The world inhabited by the *Konjaku* compiler was, as I have noted, not a safe one. Not only were there a host of social problems, such as lawlessness, to contend with, but there were also spirits which could prove dangerous to human beings. A good example of tales dealing with this sort of unusual situation is XXVII.41, the story of a fox that was in the habit of transforming itself into a young woman, begging a ride on the backs of men's horses, then jumping off and laughing at the man it had tricked.

In this tale a palace guard decides he will put an end to this practice and goes himself to the area where it has been happening. The woman appears and asks for a ride, which he provides. He then seizes and binds her. He rides back to the capital, passing various familiar landmarks, and takes the fox/woman to his fellow palace guards, who crowd about for a look.

The woman then assumes her true fox shape and runs away, and the man finds he has been duped, the victim of an elaborate illusion: what he thought was the capital and the lights of the city have been created by the fox, and in reality he is in the forest without his horse.

He goes back a second time after recovering from an illness caused by the first attempt, and this time he is successful. He threatens to burn the fox/woman and releases her after warning her not to repeat her acts. Later he returns to the area one more time and sees a young woman, to whom he offers a ride; she replies, "I don't want to be burned!" and disappears.

The compiler comments on this tale, "This must surely have happened recently. . . . Thinking of this, we can see that it has been common since antiquity for foxes to transform themselves into humans."

This, then, is an unusual event, but it is clearly instructive. Although the supernatural forces surrounding humans were superior in many ways, they were not totally superior to man, and it was thought to be possible for man to triumph in a showdown. To do so, however, required dedication and a quick wit, both of which are demonstrated by the hero of this story.

It was necessary to be on one's guard at all times, and the stories in the secular volumes should, I believe, be read as a set of instructions on how to deal with the various and frequently unforeseeable dangers of the world. As such they fit easily into the overall editorial plan of *Konjaku Monogatari-shū*.

Let us now briefly turn our attention to the editorial process itself and examine how the compiler used various sources in the making of his collection.

Sources, Unity, and Language

Each of the three topics to be considered under this heading is extremely complex and cannot be treated fully here. The compiler's use of sources, his use of language, and the structural unity of his work are interconnected. I will outline these issues and attempt to show how they bear on any approach—critical or scholarly—to *Konjaku.*

It goes without saying that the *Konjaku* compiler made liberal use of written sources in his work. We will never know the exact extent to which the individual tales in *Konjaku* are dependent on such sources, because so many of the *setsuwa* collections from the period are no longer extant, but we can point to certain tendencies with a fair amount of confidence.

In general, the compiler made far greater use of written sources in the compilation of the first ten volumes than he did in putting together the Japanese stories, but he has not used the sources in the same way in the Indian and Chinese sections, and it is worth examining some of the differences.

Each of the 185 stories in the first five volumes of the collection is presumed to have been taken from a written source. A total of eleven works—five of which are sutras—is the primary group of these written sources, but the compiler has also drawn from several other works as well, and we must conclude that he was extremely well read in the traditional Buddhist literature, and in other areas as well. [12]

In the case of the Indian stories the compiler has gone through thousands of tales and has selected for inclusion those which best suited his own purposes; further, he has followed the text rather loosely in most cases. He generally is true to the outline of the plot of his source, but seems seldom to have paid much attention to its exact wording. Some of his changes may be due to mis-understandings of the Chinese texts, but most appear to have been made deliberately.

This would not be so noticeable if it were also true for the Chinese stories, but here the plan is somewhat different. The compiler uses fewer separate sources in the Chinese tales—a total of four major and eleven less important works, as compared with eleven and nineteen for the Indian volumes—but he has followed them far more closely. Comparisons of the stories in *Konjaku* with their Chinese counterparts reveal few major changes.

Let us reconsider, for a moment, the story I translated from the Indian volumes, V.8, which, it will be remembered, is about a king who gives his head to a neighboring king. In *Konjaku*, we have the following passage:

The king of the neighboring country heard about this and in order to kill King Daikō Myōō, he hired a fortuneteller, instructing him to go to King Daikō Myōō and ask for his head.

In the source for this story—a Chinese collection of miracle tales called *Ching-lü I-hsiang*—we have the following:

Now the enemy king was a wrathful man. He heard of the king's vow and jealousy grew in his heart. He thus gathered all his ministers and asked who would go seeking the king's head, telling them the reward would be one thousand cash.

The source is more dramatic and more apt to capture the attention of the reader or listener than is the *Konjaku* treatment in this case. The compiler has pared his narrative to eliminate all but the most necessary references to persons other than the hero of the tale. The effect is to place more emphasis on the nobility of the hero by removing narrative distractions, but it is difficult to say that this was the compiler's intention. In any event, the source has the more interesting and exciting narrative.

This method is common throughout the Indian tales, but is not, as a rule, applied in the Chinese section of the collection. Here the compiler follows the texts more faithfully, and makes changes which appear calculated to enhance the literary affect of the story,[13] but does not boil the tales down the way he often does in the first five volumes.

The one major change made by the compiler consistently in volumes VI to X is that he nearly always adds a moral to the end of the story. For example, in VII.3 we learn of an old woman who has such an aversion to Buddhism that she refuses to go near Buddhist temples and even averts her eyes when she sees a monk on the road. Through a strange chain of circumstances she repeats a chant she has heard—"Praise be to the Han'ya Sutra"—and is reborn in a Buddhist heaven.

The tale ends with the following moral:

What can we learn from this? The virtues of having the Han'ya Sutra reach your ears—even though you might have hated it—are such as these. Thus it is said that how much greater, indeed, must be the virtues of accepting the Sutra with a willing heart and having it copied!

As is nearly always the case, the addition of the moral here is a part of the compiler's editorial plan. The story in question is part of the praise volumes, and the moral underscores the power and the glory of the Han'ya Sutra, which the tale is praising. In most instances the morals function in such a way. This is particularly important in the cases where the *Konajku* compiler has elected to ignore the moral in his source and add one of his own, for it shows the consistency with which he followed his editorial plan.

Why the compiler has followed his sources so much more closely in the Chinese section than in the Indian is a matter of conjecture. If the Indian tales are considered to have been included in the text largely for background, one might surmise that they were not considered as "important" as the Chinese stories, and that therefore they were treated in a more cursory manner than were the Chinese and Japanese tales. It is also possible that he felt an obligation to follow the sources more closely in the Chinese case because he assumed that his audience would have been more familiar with the story as it appeared in the source, while the Indian tales would have been much less familiar to a Heian Japanese audience.

In any event, he also follows written sources fairly closely in the Japanese volumes, and uses even fewer of them in these two sections than he had in the Chinese section. Many of the tales in these last twenty-one volumes appear to have been taken from oral tradition, and the compiler has used no more than five written sources a significant number of times. It must be remembered, of course, that many of the tales *might* have been taken from some now-lost written work, specifically the elusive *Uji Dainagon Monogatari,* but we cannot be sure about this.

Chief among the known written sources for the Japanese volumes are *Nihon Ryōiki, Dai-Nihon Hokke Genki,* and *Nihon Ōjō Gokuraku Ki.* The compiler also used a collection of miracle tales about the Bodhisattva Jizō and another one about the Bodhisattva Kannon.

The secular volumes, it might be noted, contain a much smaller number of tales which can be traced directly to written sources.

The written sources for *Konjaku* have proven among the most important evidence cited by scholars who attempt to date the collection, to name the author, or to understand its structural unity. We have already seen, for example, how Katayose used the Chinese collection *Hung-tsan Fa-hua Ch'uan* and the monk Kakujū's role in the dissemination of this work in setting a possible date for *Konjaku*.

Konjaku is thought by many to contain two "halves," the first of which (volumes I to XX) is "Buddhist" and the second of which is "secular." The fact that both Buddhist and secular volumes coexist in the same collection has proven a difficulty to any scholar who would maintain that *Konjaku* is a unified whole, and several theories have been advanced to demonstrate the collection's unity.

Among the most imaginative of these is that of Kawaguchi Hisao, which centers around a Chinese Buddhist collection of about 668 called *Fa-yüan Chu-lin*. Katayose had already held that this work is important to the development of *Konjaku* not only for the large number of tales it provided—he finds 121 stories in *Konjaku* directly or indirectly related to *Fa-yüan*[14]—but also for the influence it had on the overall structure of *Konjaku*.

Fa-yüan Chu-lin contains a total of one hundred volumes, each of which deals with a separate category of Buddhism, such as the six levels of existence. Each volume is further broken down, with each of the one hundred chapters being divided into three main sections. These are "definitions," "explications," and "appreciations." The respective roles of these three sections are to state the topic central to the chapter, to quote from sutras and commentaries concerning the topic, and to provide examples about how the topic is important in daily life. This third part often utilizes stories taken from Chinese life.

Konjaku draws from fifty-one of the one hundred chapters, and almost all of *Konjaku's* adaptations are contained in its first ten volumes. Katayose believes that the structure of the work had a good deal of influence on Japanese Buddhist collections, with

Konjaku being influenced most greatly by the third sections of the *Fa-yüan* chapters, and other works being influenced by other sections.[15]

Kawaguchi, then, theorizes that *Konjaku*'s secular tales can be compared in scope and function to the "appreciations" sections found in each *Fa-yüan* volume. The secular volumes, Kawaguchi says, were meant to show the "world of red dust" in all its reality, as a world which should be forsaken. He concludes that the secular tales were collected as "one part of the Buddhist tales; and they have a close relationship with the Buddhist stories."[16]

The reason for the mixing of secular and Buddhist tales in *Konjaku Monogatari-shū*, according to Kawaguchi, is that *Konjaku* was used, much like *Fa-yüan*, as "a source book for sermons for monks."[17] Thus Kawaguchi has found a unity of purpose in *Konjaku*, and sees the collection as having a logic and consistency in its structure.

This is clearly a step beyond much other criticism, which often tends to find unity in the very disunity of the work. One scholar, for example, finds *Konjaku* to be comprised of two halves, with the first half championing the "old" Buddhism and the "old" social values, and the second half celebrating the "new" Buddhism and a "new medieval revolutionary consciousness."[18]

The structure found by Kunisaki Fumimaro—that each major section of the work contains stories of history, praise, and didacticism—also suggests an overall unity in the work, and one that is based more on internal principles than is Kawaguchi's. Kunisaki does not agree that *Fa-yüan Chu-lin* was as important in the formulation of *Konjaku* as Katayose or Kawaguchi have claimed, but turns instead to two other Chinese collections, *San-pao Kan-ying Yao Lüeh-lu* and *Ming-pao Chi*.[19]

San-pao is a work of 162 tales, and of these Kunisaki finds a total of seventy-two represented, either directly or indirectly, in *Konjaku*. Most are in volumes VI and VII. He makes a great deal out of the fact that the *Konjaku* compiler sometimes preserved the order of the tales he adapted from *San-pao*, even though he did not do so with the stories from *Fa-yüan*. He also finds it significant that *San-pao*, a work in three volumes, is centered around the "three treasures," which we have seen are also important in the praise sections of *Konjaku*.

However one judges the validity of any of these attempts to find unity in the structure of *Konjaku,* it is significant to note that all serious attempts have found it necessary to make use of the Chinese Buddhist sources of this Japanese collection. In the light of this scholarly agreement it is particularly difficult to understand how anyone could fail to agree that the compiler of *Konjaku* was, if not a Buddhist monk, at the very least a person well versed in Buddhist literature.

The *Konjaku* sources are used to explain more than the organization of the collection, however. Linguists have long studied *Konjaku,* and have noted in particular striking differences between the language of the Buddhist and the secular tales; there have even been theories that two halves were the products of two different compilers.[20]

It is generally agreed, however, that the major reason for the differences in writing style and language is not that there were separate compilers, but rather that the tales in the first twenty volumes have a high percentage of sources which were written in Chinese—this is true even of many of the Japanese Buddhist tales, which were based on collections composed in Japan but in the Chinese language—while the sources for the Japanese secular stories tend to be either oral tradition in Japan or sources which were written in Japanese.[21]

This may well be true, but my own study shows that the function of the stories may play a larger role than has been acknowledged in the language used by the compiler. For example, the language of the didactic volumes XIX and XX is more colloquial than that of the other Buddhist tales, even though volume XX, in particular, contains many stories based on *Nihon Ryōiki,* a work which was written in Chinese.[22]

To briefly recapitulate, then, it is clear that the sources of *Konjaku Monogatari-shū* must be viewed as having provided more than the wording or the plot outline of many of the collection's tales. There is some dependence on sources for the language in the individual stories, and it is possible that the sources have even influenced the structure of the work.

Clearly *Konjaku Monogatari-shū* is a vast work which contains such a variety of tales that it is impossible to make any easy generalizations about it. It stands at the fountainhead of its own tradition—that of *setsuwa* literature in Japan—and apparently borrows greatly from Chinese traditions as well. Let us now turn our attention to its position in the literary history of Japan.

Chapter Four
Konjaku Monogatari-shū in Japanese Literature

Konjaku Monogatari-shū is a collection made primarily for the education and salvation of its readers, but at the same time it shares many traits with those collections intended for entertainment, and it therefore occupies an important place in the history of Japanese *setsuwa* literature. The *setsuwa* genre is but one of the many which have flourished in Japan, however, and it is now time to see how *Konjaku* fits into the overall picture of Japanese literature.

This chapter will deal with two major points. The first of these will be general: I will attempt to clarify the position of *setsuwa* and *setsuwa* literature in Japanese literature in general. The second is more concrete, involving a comparative discussion of *Konjaku Monogatari-shū,* in an effort to see its differences and similarities to other Japanese literary works.

For the purpose of convenience in this latter task I will deal with three primary areas: *Konjaku* in Heian literature, *Konjaku* in medieval literature, and *Konjaku* in modern Japanese literature.

Setsuwa in Japanese Literature

If modern scholars have been reluctant to treat *setsuwa* as literature it must be admitted that they are in good company, for there is no indication that they were thought of as "literature" at the time most of the *setsuwa* collections were being made. Documents from the Heian period yield scant information about the existence or acceptance of individual collections, though we get an occasional reference in one collection to the existence of earlier ones.

It must be remembered that *setsuwa* were not identified with the word "setsuwa" until the modern period, so it is sometimes difficult to be sure just how a Heian audience might have perceived stories we now label *setsuwa*. *Setsuwa* are one kind of story, and if we look back to the Heian period to see what the average reader thought of when he heard the word "story" we begin to make some progress.

It is obvious that the Heian and Kamakura Japanese had a strong consciousness of the existence of at least two types of stories, these being fabricated tales *(tsukuri-monogatari)* and true stories. The true stories were of several different varieties and included those tales we now call *setsuwa*. This is made clear in an early Kamakura work of literary criticism called *Mumyō Zōshi*.

In this work an old nun—who is the voice of the author—has been holding forth on the merits of various sections of *Genji Monogatari* and other court romances when she is asked to comment on *Ise Monogatari* and *Yamato Monogatari*. The questioner says that such works as these must be especially valuable because they are true and not manufactured.

We have already seen that the author of *Sambō E Kotoba* had a similar opinion; he condemns the romances in no uncertain terms because they represent things which were not true. The author of the Heian diary *Kagerō Nikki* also calls the court romances "rank fabrications," though it is not certain that she disapproves of them as strongly as she pretends.

Setsuwa, then, fall into this category of true tales. Since all tales are referred to as *monogatari*, it would appear that the Heian and Kamakura Japanese had not developed their genre consciousness to the point where such distinctions could be made, even though they made them when they discussed tales in general. The stories we now call *setsuwa* differed from other true stories mainly in their purpose, if at all. There is an alarming tendency on the part of modern scholars to label only those stories contained in *setsuwa* collections as *setsuwa*, thus ignoring the fact that remarkably similar tales exist in other contexts where they are labeled as something entirely different. For example, we call the narrative prefaces to some of the poems in poetry anthologies *kotobagaki,* and the narratives found in *Ise Monogatari uta mono-gatari,* when in point of fact both types of narratives are also found in *Konjaku Monogatari-shū,* where we call them *setsuwa.*

In our attempt to understand *setsuwa* literature and how it developed alongside other genres in Japan, then, we should turn briefly to a consideration of *monogatari,* for, as I have noted, all stories were called by this name.

The word *monogatari* is now translated as "story," but Mitani Eiichi holds that it originally had very different connotations. The word is made up of two different parts: *mono* means "thing," and *gatari* is derived from the verb *kataru,* meaning "to tell" or "to relate." The word *mono* had a very different meaning in ancient Japan, however. Then it meant "spirit," or "ghost." The *mono* was an evil spirit, one that did evil work in the world of men; this opposes it to the *kami,* or deity, which was by and large good.[1] People with some link to the other world were known as *monoshiri,* or "those who know the *mono.*"

The oldest stories in Japan are associated with the foundation of the most important clans. Many of them were told as a matter of belief, depicting as they did the clan's origin as being the result of some kind of union between a mortal and a deity. Examples of this would include stories about the thunder deity and women who had sexual intercourse with snakes. These stories were often called *katarigoto,* or "told things," or *furugoto,* which means "old things." But as the stories were told outside of the immediate family circles they gradually grew apart from the belief which spawned them and were told as miracle tales, or stories associated with the supernatural in a general way; hence the name *monogatari,* or "stories about dangerous spirits," became common.

This particular explanation then traces the path of literary development from belief to fiction, holding that the *setsuwa* were an outgrowth of the *monogatari,* and remained closer to actual belief than did the *monogatari. Monogatari,* in short, were about events which were no longer believed, and hence were fiction in the eyes of the Heian and Kamakura readership; *setsuwa,* on the other hand, were true stories. According to Mitani, by the eleventh century there was no longer any connection between *setsuwa* and *monogatari*, despite their common origins.

It seems paradoxical to say that stories regarded as true were valued more highly than those which were regarded as false while at the same time *setsuwa* (also stories thought to be true) were not considered as literature at all. However, the drive to produce a "true" literature is remarkable throughout Heian literature and will give us a number of points of comparison with *setsuwa*. Let us turn, then, to an examination of Heian literature and *Konjaku*'s position in it.

Konjaku in Heian Literature

A general consciousness of genre developed in the Heian period (795–1186), and this consciousness informs the entire literary production of the era. It should be stressed that the bulk of Heian literature was written for aristocrats by aristocrats; the most highly valued form of literary expression to these aristocrats was poetry, and it is not surprising to find that genres seem to grow out of their various connections with poetics. The first of a long string of imperially commissioned poetry anthologies, the *Kokin Waka-shū* [Collection of Old and New Verse in Japanese], was produced in 905. It is safe to say that nearly all of the members of the aristocratic classes both read and wrote poetry frequently.

The form used almost exclusively in the court was the *waka* ("Japanese poem," to distinguish it from poetry in Chinese), also know as *tanka* ("short poem"), a lyrical verse form composed of a total of thirty-one syllables, divided into five lines with five, seven, five, seven, and seven syllables, respectively. This is a very dense form which makes use of a high degree of convention, frequent puns, and the use of associative words which call to mind a season or some other image to the educated reader. To fully appreciate a *tanka* one needs to have been educated in the same way that the *tanka* writer would have been educated, which is of course an impossible task for the modern reader, be she Japanese or Western.

It is important to keep in mind that there is virtually no tradition of narrative poetry in Japan. This obviously has implications for the later development of prose fiction in Japan, for there was no tradition of stories with well-defined plots. Japanese prose fiction tends to be lyrical, placing more importance on theme than on plot, which sometimes makes it difficult for the Western reader to cope with; tension and resolution, so important to the Westerner, were conceived of in different terms by Japanese writers.

There are three important forms of prose fiction associated with the Heian period, all of which have some ties to poetry. These are the diary, the romance, and the *setsuwa*. In the pages that follow I will discuss the romance and the diary in terms of their similarities to and differences from *setsuwa*, referring in particular to *Konjaku Monogatari-shū*. My concern will be to show that *Konjaku* is closer to the so-called mainstream of Heian literature than it is usually considered to be by those studies which focus largely on aesthetic, courtly literature.

Since poetry stands at the core of this literary tradition, then, let us proceed to a consideration of the nature of Heian poetry, focusing on the problems which the poets most often addressed themselves to and the methods by which they expressed themselves.

Poetry and Poetry Collections. The poetry written in Heian Japan was filled with various types of literary convention, a fact which is not surprising when we note that it was written by aristocrats for aristocrats, and that nearly all Heian aristocrats received extensive training in poetry. This poetry training generally took the form of memorizing the bulk of previously written poetry and copying its style, a practice which clearly would promote skillful use of convention since the poet could be certain her readers would catch her meaning if it were couched in conventional language. The *tanka* is only thirty-one syllables in length, and Japanese is a polysyllabic language, so the average *tanka* contains a total of from seven to nine words. The use of puns and other wordplays was of great importance to Heian poets because it allowed them to pack a greater amount of content into their poetry than would have otherwise been possible. Heian poetry is seldom direct, and frequently it is up to the reader to interpret a poem from clues provided by the poet. The second poem in the *Kokin Waka-shū* will demonstrate this. The poet is Ki Tsurayuki (884–946), one of the most famous of the Heian poets:

> My sleeves wet,
> the water I've gathered there
> is still frozen—
> but today, the first spring day,
> surely the wind will thaw us.

"Wet sleeves" is a frequent image in Heian literature and would have been immediately familiar to the contemporary reader; it is generally taken to mean the tears shed by a lover whose love is not requited. While the poem appears on the surface to be celebrating the coming of spring, the wet sleeves suggest that it might have been a love poem. This possibility is buttressed by the use of two other words, those I have translated as "gathered" and "thaw." The word for "gathered" in this case is *musubu* which can also mean "to tie," or "to make a relationship." It is followed by its logical antithesis, the word *tōkeru,* which in addition to meaning "to thaw" can also mean "untie" and "to grow intimate." So the poem suggests that the male poet wishes some lady who had not been returning his feelings to thaw out and grow more intimate with him.

As is generally the case with the lyric, this meaning is more or less buried in the poem and must be uncovered by the reader. The Heian poet apparently felt that one had very little chance of stating truth directly, and generally attempted to arrive at it through a more circuitous route. One way of accomplishing this was to make use of dualities such as *musubu* and *tōkeru* with their meanings of "tie" and "untie"; another was to juxtapose images. The educated reader would of course appreciate Tsurayuki's effort for its technical achievements as well as for whatever deeper meaning she read into it; the poem is truly a "well-wrought urn," with every image working to create a pleasing whole.

Anothe poem by Tsurayuki will demonstrate further the approach used in the Heian period:

> The mist is rising
> and from the trees the buds spring
> snow is still falling—
> even the flowerless village
> has become flower-covered.

Here we have the "elegant confusion" so often used in Heian poetry—although the poet's knowledge tells him one thing his eyes tell him something else, and the result is a thorough confusion as to the nature of reality. Flowers and snow are especially popular in this type of poem. Tsurayuki makes use of a skillful pun—the word *haru* in Japanese can mean either "spring" (as the season) or "to swell" (as buds on trees swell, in this case)—to draw his separate realities together. The mist and flowers are rising, the snow falling, and the poet is caught somewhere in the middle. The poetic posture is one of hopeless confusion, of total inability to distinguish which of the poet's two "realities" is the more real.

Thus the Heian poet probes his world in a delicate search for the true meaning of things. He is caught up in a sort of dream world, where intuition often seems to have more validity than the senses. The poetry of the times almost inevitably utilizes nature—the changing of the seasons was especially important as a poetic topic—but it is seldom a totally objective nature, for the poet's feelings, interpretations and basic doubts creep into nearly every natural setting.

The *Konjaku* compiler is not insensitive to these questions.[2] One story which trades on this theme is XIX. 11, the tale about the conversion of the "Watō Kannon."[3] In this story a villager is informed by a dream that the Kannon will pay a visit to the hot springs where he lives, and when the man—a hunter who has injured his arm in an accident—arrives, the villagers place more faith in the dream than they do in their own senses. Eventually the man himself comes to believe that his outward appearance is but an illusion and that he must indeed be the Kannon, and he converts to Buddhism on the spot.

The question we are left with concerns the nature of "reality"—
to what extent can we trust our senses when we attempt to say
what is real? Could it be that all people are like the hunter,
resembling humble mortals on the outside and carrying within
them the soul of a Bodhisattva which cannot manifest itself because of our refusal to acknowledge the reality of that which we
cannot see? Questions such as this were important to the *Konjaku*
compiler, as they were to the poets of the Heian period.

The question of reality and illusion was often used in a hu-
morous way by the compiler of *Konjaku* and other *setsuwa* collections in addition to the more serious manner described above.
A story which comes to mind is XX.3, which describes how the
Buddha once manifested himself in a large persimmon tree in the
capital. This naturally attracted great crowds and the Buddha
responded like a true showman, emitting a golden light and
showering the onlookers with flowers. A government minister
heard about the miracle and was suspicious; knowing that such
magic is only effective for seven days, he went on the seventh in
full court attire and stared at the Buddha for some two hours.
The longer he stared, the more uncomfortable the "Buddha"
obviously became. Finally he tumbled out of the tree in his true
shape, a scavenger bird. The minister concluded that the people
had been foolish to be taken in so easily by a tengu, a type of
superhuman creature that is said to be very fond of playing tricks
on mortals.

There are also stories in *Konjaku* about foxes which transform
themselves and deceive people, in addition to various other stories
with similar motifs.

It is clear that questions regarding the nature of reality and
illusion were common ones in Heian Japan, and the mere fact
that they are taken up by both poets and the compilers of *setsuwa*
collections such as *Konjaku* does not necessarily show that the
Konjaku compiler was influenced by poetry. We can, however,
compare the treatment of the idea as it is found in both poetry
and *Konjaku* and when we do so we will find that both use this
common idea that illusion and reality are often difficult to distinguish to make suggestive statements about the nature of truth.

There is a more concrete link between *Konjaku* and Heian poetry than the fact that each makes use of identical themes on occasion, however, which I would like to take up at this point. This link centers around the editorial techniques found in many of the imperially sponsored poetry anthologies and the technique used to link stories together in *Konjaku*.

Poems are arranged in anthologies according to a principle which Konishi, Brower, and Miner have called "progression and integration."[4] To see what this means let us consider briefly the case of the *Kokinshū*, the first imperial anthology produced in Japan, completed in 905. The first six of this anthology's twenty volumes contain poems about the seasons, and they are arranged in seasonal order in the anthology. That is, the first two volumes contain spring poems, the third contains summer poems, the fourth and fifth contain poems about autumn, and the sixth contains winter poems. Furthermore, the poems within each individual volume proceed in a chronological manner. The first spring poem, for example, is set on the first day of spring, and the last is on the last day of spring. If we read the seasonal poems in order, then, we will proceed through the year practically day by day.

Within this overall setting we go from image group to image group. To take the case of the first fifteen poems in the first volume of the *Kokinshū* as an example, the first poem sets the general tone of the group (significantly, it is a poem questioning the nature of the poet's reality); poems 2 to 4 emphasize moisture and thawing; 6 to 9 are about "elegant confusion" which arises from the uncertainty as to whether the poet has seen snow or flowers; 10 and 11 use sound imagery; 12 to 14 are about natural images associated with the coming of spring, such as the wind; and 15 shifts to imagery of fragrance.

Hence the organization of the poems was important to Ki Tsurayuki, the *Kokinshū* compiler, for he used the poems as a set of building blocks in the creation of the collection. The collection itself takes on an artistic identity through such arrangement.

The *Konjaku* compiler did much the same thing with the *setsuwa* he selected for his collection. We have already seen how he has grouped his stories into geographical units and how within these geographical units he arranges stories according to whether they are historical, laudatory, or didactic tales. In addition to this organization, however, the compiler used another principle to link tales together within individual volumes.

This technique has been identified by Kunisaki Fumimaro, who has labeled it *ni wa, ichi rui,* or "two stories, one type."[5] In essence, the editorial plan described by Kunisaki works as follows: story A is linked by some kind of concrete imagery (often a place name or the like) to story B; stories C and D are linked in a similar fashion; and story B is linked in yet another way to story C. The result is that the stories are arranged in obvious pairs, and that the pairs themselves are linked together, but in a different way, so that in the sequence of A, B, C, and D, for example, A and C have no links between them. The stories flow smoothly forward as a result of this type of arrangement. Although the links are generally concrete, there are some thematic ones as well, and one finds that each volume in *Konjaku* is an integrated whole.[6]

Kunisaki seems to believe that this *ni wa, ichi rui* principle must have come from China, since he found no precedents for it in Japan,[7] but I would suggest that the arrangement of the poems in the *Kokinshū* and subsequent imperial poetry anthologies is the precedent. This type of editorial work is particularly effective because it allows one to appreciate the individual poems, or stories in the case of *Konjaku,* both as individual works and as parts of a larger whole. However one wishes to understand the relationship here, it is clear that both the overall organization of stories into groups and the linkings between stories that we find in *Konjaku* would not have been especially foreign to anyone familiar with the poetry anthologies.

Thus we can see the *Konjaku* does have some ties to the so-called mainstream of Heian literature. The *Konjaku* editorial method, in any event, would have been recognized as artistic by a contemporary audience. The fact that such a method was used gives further credence to the theory that *Konjaku* was intended for an aristocratic audience.

Let us now turn to a consideration of the diary, one of the most uniquely Japanese of the Heian genres and one which seems to bridge the gap between prose and poetry.

The Poetic Diary. The question of precisely what *nikki bungaku* ("diary literature") is has yet to be answered definitively by scholars. Works placed in the general classification are quite diverse, and there has been no study of the genre which seeks to clarify what structural aspects are common to all the works placed within it. The general scholarly approach has been an external one—it is customary to call those works thought to have been drawn from the lives of their authors "diaries" and not to deal with the specific form those "diaries" take. Scholarly debate about classification has developed when it is not certain whether the work in question was indeed taken from the life of its author (or, for that matter, whether its supposed author is really the author); the result has been the creation of a gray area of works such as *Takamura Monogatari, Heichū Monogatari,* or even *Izumi Shikibu Nikki,* which are classified or not classified as *nikki* depending on the opinions of individual scholars.

Interestingly enough the first two of the above have also been studied by *setsuwa* scholars, a fact which demonstrates how important "truth" is in *setsuwa.*

It is possible to speak of the form of the diary as long as we do not lose sight of the fact that any such remarks are apt to be rather general in nature. It is commonly noted that there were two types of diary kept in Heian Japan—those written in Chinese by men, and those in Japanese by women. The diaries of the men were official or semiofficial documents, and the more literary diaries of the women were born from them. In order to understand diary literature, then, it is necessary to have some knowledge of these preliterary diaries kept by men.

An examination of the extant diaries kept by various court noblemen will reveal that they have a primary allegiance to the recording of facts but that they sometimes add a fair amount of private commentary to the record. The writers of the more literary diaries, however, recorded only those aspects of their lives they felt were important to some general aesthetic pattern which gave meaning to their lives and as such are much more interpretative works.

So both the preliterary diary associated with men and the literary diary associated with women begin with the idea of recording the truth and grow from there. The men's diaries keep close to this objective although the personality of the diarist is frequently evident; the women's diaries, on the other hand, are really poetic retrospectives which look back on the diarist's life and attempt to interpret it for the audience. This is a search for meaning, and not a random recording of facts. Facts which do not fit the pattern are simply omitted and one feels that works such as *Sarashina Nikki* (translated into English as "As I Crossed a Bridge of Dreams," more literally understood simply as "Sarashina Diary," Sarashina being a place name) were actually written in their entirety toward the end of the diarist's life from notes she had kept or from memory, rather than being recorded on a daily basis throughout her life.

It is this preoccupation with the idea of truth that really provides the link between *setsuwa* and diaries. The preliterary diary in particular is event-centered, and is often kept with the purpose of recording actual events for the education of later generations. In the diary *Chūyūki,* kept by Fujiwara Munetada, for example, we find frequent references to searches among old documents for precedents for actions which have been proposed. Both the transmitter of a *setsuwa* and the keeper of a diary had a basic interest in facts, both for the sake of the facts themselves and for what could be learned from them.

If the preliterary diary has as its aim the recording of events as they happened, the literary diary is more interested in the meaning of individual events. The writer of a Heian poetic diary was concerned primarily with providing her readers with an interpretative history of her life and thus selected the events she would describe and manipulated them within the diary for maximum poetic effect. Much as the poet described nature in a very subjective way the diarist was subjective about her life.

On one level, much the same could be said about the compiler of *Konjaku Monogatari-shū* and his use of individual *setsuwa*. While he was careful to choose stories which would be of interest to his readers, he was more concerned about how the stories demonstrated some deeper truth: the stories were but means to a greater end. Like the diarist, the *Konjaku* compiler worked to establish his truth through selectivity—choosing the right story for the right place—and through manipulation of the story within his collection.

The poetic diary and *setsuwa* collections like *Konjaku,* then, have in common the fact that they both originate in the impulse to record events, but go beyond that impulse and involve themselves in the exploration of the meanings of events. In any case they have the ring of truth to them and it is not surprising that both the editor of a *setsuwa* collection and the writer of a poetic diary condemned the romances roundly as being "rank fabrications," stories unfit for decent folks to read because they were untrue.[8]

The *Monogatari* Genres.   There are three main types of *monogatari* that I will discuss here. The first and most common of these is the so-called *tsukuri monogatari* (romance), which was generally fabricated and held by some to be unfit to read; the second is the *uta monogatari* (poem tale); and the third is the *rekishi monogatari* (history tale). The latter two are really quite different from the *tsukuri monogatari* because they are associated with history and considered to be factual. We will begin with the poem tale.

The best-known poem tale collection is *Ise Monogatari* [Tales of Ise], whose episodes generally turn around the life of the famous Ariwara Narihira (825–880), who was known especially for his skill as a poet and his reputation as a lover. The episodes in *Ise* begin with Narihira's birth and end with his death; in between we have some attempt at chronology but the episodes by no means constitute a sustained narrative. The work in most of its manuscripts contains 125 episodes, most of which are short and contain at least one poem.

Some of these poems are attributed to Narihira and others are of unknown origin, but the work by and large allows a glimpse at Narihira's career. Although we do not know who actually wrote the work, it seems clear that he had access to Narihira's own private poetry collection. The work was probably produced in the early tenth century.

It is thought by some scholars that works like *Ise* (and it should be pointed out that there are very few works like *Ise* extant) probably had their origins in public and private poetry anthologies. When poems were put into public anthologies they were sometimes accompanied by headnotes which purported to explain the circumstances under which they were composed. The private collections as well would often note the circumstances of composition and sometimes would include a reply to the poem if an interesting one was made.

Since Japanese poetry is often occasional, a lyrical response to some event, these headnotes were necessary to understand the poem. Some of them are rather long and constitute stories in their own right, and it is this kind of story-poem combination which by and large makes up works like *Ise Monogatari*. As an illustration, consider the following:

Once when Narihira had gone to the province of Ise he met very secretly with the woman who was the Ise Shrine Virgin. On the following day he had no way of sending a message to her and was languishing in his thoughts when the following arrived from the woman. Poet unknown.

> You came to me?
> Or did I go to you?
> I cannot think . . .
> Was it dream? Reality?
> Was I sleeping? Awake?

The above is from the *Kokinshū* (poem 645, one of the love poems). It is also the basic story which was adapted as episode 69 of *Ise*, where it reads as follows:

Once there was a man. This man went to the province of Ise as an Imperial Huntsman. The parent of the woman who was serving in the Ise Shrine sent word, "Treat this person better than you would an ordinary messenger," and because it was the will of her parent, she treated him very kindly. In the morning he went out to hunt, and when it became evening he returned, and she had him come to her quarters. This is how politely she treated him.

On the evening of the second day of his stay the man unexpectedly said, "I wish to meet you tonight." Now the woman had herself no great aversion to such a meeting. There were many people around, however, and she was unable to arrange a meeting. Because he was not an ordinary messenger he was staying close to her room and since his room was close to the woman's sleeping quarters, when people had gone to sleep that night she went to his room around the middle of the night.

The man was not sleeping, but lying there looking outside when by the faint light of the moon he saw a person enter his room with a small servant girl ahead of her. The man was very happy at this and pulled her to where he was lying. She stayed from eleven o'clock until about two. She went back to her own room without making any pledges, however. This made the man very sad, and he could not sleep.

At dawn he was worrying about the woman but there was no one he could send to her and he had to wait restlessly. Shortly after it grew light the following poem came from the woman without any note:

> You came to me?
> Or did I go to you?
> I cannot think . . .
> Was it dream? Reality?
> Was I sleeping? Awake?

This episode then goes on to record the man's response and some further details about the relationship.[9]

It was long assumed that the man in this story was, as the headnote to the *Kokinshū* poem says, Narihira, but there is no particular evidence to support this assumption.[10] The entire episode seems to have been written on the basis of the poems and the brief headnote in the *Kokinshū*.

This episode is different from the *setsuwa* we find in *Konjaku Monogatari-shū* in that it contains no reference to any Buddhist moral. It also contains a total of three poems. There are, of course, stories in *Konjaku* which do contain poems, and there are also secular stories which have no Buddhist moral (although they do generally have some sort of conclusion or final remark by the compiler); hence it is difficult to point to any specific way that this episode differs in kind from those we find in *Konjaku*. Poem tales of the sort quoted above are stories which are short, based on some event thought to have happened, and were often transmitted by word of mouth. The same could be said of many *setsuwa*. There are, in fact, three stories in *Konjaku* apparently based on episodes in *Ise*.[11]

Although *Ise* is called a *monogatari* and fits Mitani's definition of *monogatari* as tales which originated to explain the growth of clans and eventually grew separate from the beliefs which spawned them, it has no apparent connection with the supernatural. Mitani explains this by arguing that the name *Ise Monogatari* is a later invention and that the tales included in the work were not originally a part of the *katarigoto* tradition.[12] Obviously not all of the earliest stories dealt mainly with the supernatural—interspersed among the supernatural tales were others which were more in celebration of the achievements of human culture.

According to Mitani, the telling of stories grew first out of a split between men and the deities with the stories being to some degree an affirmation of human culture.[13] If this is indeed the case then the episodes we find in *Ise*, I would postulate, are affirmations of the culture of the group in which they were produced; their main goal is to celebrate the cultural attainments (in this case the writing of poetry) of people like Narihira, who then became symbolic of all that is good in human culture. It is important to keep in mind the fact that the aesthetic literature of the Heian court is not without its links to the oral tradition of the court.

By celebrating the cultural attainments of a real member of society *Ise* serves as an educational work. It offers an education to aspiring poets, for it shows the kinds of poems which are appropriate—and sometimes those which are inappropriate—in any given situation, and it offers a model of a successful figure who is suitable for imitation by members of the work's audience. Insofar as it is an educational work, *Ise* has yet another point in common with *Konjaku*. Both of these collections provide a blueprint for life for their readers even though their respective interests and historical situations differed significantly.

An examination of a story which appears in both *Konjaku* and *Ise* will demonstrate the different concerns of the two works. The story is *Konjaku* XXX.4, which is related to *Ise* 62; in the *Ise* version this tale contains only seven lines of prose and two poems, while the *Konjaku* tale is four pages long but has only one poem. The story development is obviously more complex in *Konjaku*.

In the *Ise* story a woman leaves her husband who had neglected her for some time and takes a lowly position in the household of another man because, we are told, she is not very clever. It happens that one day she must serve food to her former husband, who recognizes her and recites a poem which is not very complimentary to her. He then recites another poem and gives her a robe but she is so embarrassed by the encounter that she runs away and is never heard of again. The story is apparently in praise of the cleverness of the former husband, and we barely see the woman.

The *Konjaku* version, however, is quite different. Here the woman is portrayed as a high ranking aristocrat who is the only child of her parents. When they die she urges her husband to move on to a more promising situation and leave her behind. He eventually complies with this request but apparently not on his own volition. The woman's existence is miserable; all of her servants have left and she lives alone in the corner of her house with virtually nothing to eat.

An old nun, who has been in the habit of bringing her food occasionally, is asked by a young man about to assume a minor post in the provinces if she will recommend a young lady servant. The nun tells him of the abandoned princess. His interest is pricked, and he eventually marries her although she refuses his first offers. Later she inadvertently encounters her former husband, whom she does not recognize. When he makes a poem that reveals his identity she dies on the spot, apparently of acute embarrassment. The *Konjaku* compiler tells us that the man was heartless and that he should not have told the woman the truth, but that he should have continued to support her financially.

As is often the case with stories dealing with aristocrats, the *Konjaku* compiler places great emphasis on the pathos of the situation and the total lack of support the woman has in the world. The tale calls to mind an earlier *Konjaku* story, XIX.5, which is also about an aristocratic woman deserted by her husband (through no fault of his own) who ends up living in a corner of her former house (which has been largely destroyed by passers-by who have used its wood for firewood) with scarcely any clothes or food and only an elderly nun to rely on. In this tale, too, the heroine dies after being reunited with her husband.

In both of these stories the heartlessness of the men involved is connected with their service in governmental positions outside the capital. This vividly demonstrates the appalling consequences of the aristocrats being forced to cope with the economic necessities of the world.

Such pathos is only infrequently depicted in *Ise Monogatari,* a work which was written during a time much less harsh than the period the *Konjaku* compiler knew. The pathos that interested the *Ise* author is of another kind, having to do with the poetic sensitivities of the hero and some of the women; it is generally resolved by the writing of a skillful poem or two. The *Ise* hero is remarkably sensitive to the nuances of his society and always is able to react in the proper way even when he has exiled himself from the court, but in *Konjaku* the source of pathos lies in the anachronistic nature of the aristocratic heroes.

It is perhaps understandable that there are very few stories which appear in both *Konjaku* and *Ise;* the two works have considerably different social backgrounds and each attempts to teach its readers how best to cope with life as the readers will find it. There are, however, a few tales from other poem tale collections such as *Yamato Monogatari* that are more concerned with the event around which the poem was composed than with the education of an audience in the niceties of poetic composition. One can observe in these cases as well remarkable differences in the treatments of the stories.

When there is something about the story behind the composition of the poem which seems appealing, the *Konjaku* compiler even makes periodic use of poetry anthologies such as the *Kokin-shū*. The following is typical of the kind of treatment he gives to the *Kokinshū* poems. Let us first look at the *Kokinshū* headnote and poem 407:

When he was exiled to the province of Oki he made this poem and, as he was boarding his boat, sent it to a person in the capital. Ono Takamura.

> The bay at Wata—
> hundreds of islands through here
> where we now row . . .
> Tell this to my lady,
> oh boats of the fishermen!

Ono Takamura (802–852) was a famous diplomat who was exiled during the course of his career. Compare the above to *Konjaku* XXIV.45, which is brief enough to translate in its entirety:

Long ago, there was a man called Ono Takamura. Something happened, and he was exiled to the province of Oki. When he got on his boat and was ready to leave he made the following poem:

> The bay at Wata—
> hundreds of islands through here
> where we now row . . .
> Tell this to my lady,
> oh boats of the fishermen!

They arrived at a place called Akashi, where they spent the night. It was the ninth month and he could not sleep in the dawn light. As he lay there sighing he saw a boat sail behind an island out of sight and was moved by this. He wrote this poem:

> Dimly, darkly
> through the Akashi bay,
> in the morning mist
> hidden by the island—
> my thoughts float with that boat.

He wept as he recited this.

It is reported that all of this was told by someone who heard Takamura tell it when he returned from his exile.

The second poem in this tale is also in the *Kokinshū* (409), but it is listed as "poet unknown." A postscript says that it has been attributed to Kakinomoto no Hitomaro, a much earlier poet. There is no indication anywhere but this *Konjaku* tale that the "Dimly, darkly" poem was written by Takamura. The poem, it should be noted, is among the best known of the *Kokinshū* poems.

As even a cursory glance at the *Konjaku* tale will show, the compiler was more interested in developing the story than in merely reporting the circumstances under which the poem was composed. He has taken these two poems which have similar imagery and put them in a common story centered around the theme of Takamura's exile. Takamura was well known in the Heian period and his exile was also famous, so the story can utilize this preexisting knowledge as background.

The *Konjaku* compiler was drawn to poems that had some story behind them which a contemporary audience would have liked for one reason or another. Parenthetically it should be noted that the compiler used at least seven poems from a later collection, the *Goshūi-shū,* which was compiled in 1086 and was likely beginning to circulate at about the same time the compiler was busy with his own work.

We must conclude that even though the *Konjaku* compiler made fairly liberal use of both poem tale collections such as *Ise* and *Yamato Monogatari* and often developed stories contained in headnotes to poems in the imperial anthologies, he was generally attracted to the tales for different reasons than were the first compilers. He expends most of his energy on depicting the situations which inspired the poems and not on the poems themselves. These situations on the whole are very sad occasions which show members of the aristocratic classes in postures of isolation and even desperation. The *Konjaku* compiler was most definitely writing for a contemporary audience, one which would have been more impressed with depictions of people in plights similar to their own.

It must be noted at this point that fragility and weakness are considered beautiful throughout Heian literature and are called *aware,* often translated as "pathos." We should not, therefore, assume that the *Konjaku* compiler had no precedent on which to base his portrayals. On the other hand, it is also true that he has taken his descriptions much further than was the custom in Heian literature.

The adaptations of the more courtly poem tales we find in *Konjaku* underscore the similarities between this genre and *setsuwa.* Such stories exist in relative abundance in *Konjaku* and are obviously not out of place there. It seems difficult to justify calling poem tales and *setsuwa* different genres, for all that really differs is the use to which the tales have been put. *Setsuwa* have been traditionally associated with Buddhism and/or popular entertainment, while *uta monogatari* have been associated with courtly aesthetics and poetry; essentially each genre is composed of legends used for the education and entertainment of a particular audience. It is the specific function of the stories and not their form which differs.

Another popular category of the *monogatari* in the Heian period was the *rekishi monogatari,* or history tale. These works began to flourish toward the end of the Heian period and continued into the Kamakura period; a common theme is a longing to return to the grandeur of the past. One of the most popular of these works is *Eiga Monogatari,* written shortly after 1107, which relates essentially the story of the Fujiwara family, the family that dominated the social and political scene for so long during the Heian period. There was also a series of works with the word "mirror" (*kagami*) in their title; these include *Ōkagami* (written after *Eiga Monogatari,* although the exact date is unknown), *Mizu Kagami* (written in the late twelfth century), and *Ima Kagami* (1170). The format taken by the works is a conversation between an old person (generally said to be well over one hundred years of age) and several younger people, with the older person telling the younger people stories from the past.

These works are episodic and based largely on oral tradition, and it is difficult to call them true histories. They are better thought of as historical romances. In any event, they have much in common with *setsuwa* collections if we speak only of form, for they are composed of short tales which clearly resemble *setsuwa,* but there is little to be said about the connection between *Konjaku Monogatari-shū* and works from this genre.

Konjaku is directed toward teaching people how to survive in the world in which they live, and the history tales have as their main purpose the recounting of the glories of the past. Thus *Konjaku* uses different types of stories in completely different ways from the history tales and this makes comparison between *Konjaku* and any work from the *rekishi monogatari* category tenuous at best. Some other tale collections, such as *Kokon Chomonjū* (1254), which fall into the category of collections intended for entertainment, have a more noticeable connection.

Only a handful of the stories in *Konjaku* have any parallels in the *rekishi monogatari,* specifically in *Ōkagami.* One of these stories is *Konjaku* XXVIII.3, which tells how an old man appeared at a poetry contest without an invitation and was evicted, becoming the butt of several jokes. The *Konjaku* version is considerably more detailed than that found in *Ōkagami* and it is difficult to say that there is any direct relationship between the texts at all. Other cases are even more tenuous, sometimes sharing only a single name. Since we do not really know when either *Konjaku* or *Ōkagami* was written it is also impossible to say that one borrowed from the other. Any tales in common would appear to be the result of oral tradition and not of copying from written texts.

The fact that *Konjaku* is so far from the history tales even though there is a basic similarity in form underscores the fact that the *Konjaku* compiler had very little interest in the past. His interests were clearly in the present.

The romance (*tsukuri monogatari*) was by far the most popular of the genres in the Heian court. It is likely that these works were read most avidly by women. There are several extant, and documents from the period refer to at least twenty-eight which have now been lost; it is likely that there were many more. In his preface to *Sambō E Kotoba* Minamoto Tamenori says that they were as numerous as pebbles on the beach or trees in the forest.

The best known of the *monogatari* extant today are *Genji Monogatari* (about 1002), *Ochikubo Monogatari* (mid-tenth century), *Utsubo Monogatari* (also read *Utsuho*, probably written in the second half of the tenth century), and *Taketori Monogatari* (the oldest extant romance, thought to have been written about 900). There are also some problematic works, such as *Takamura Monogatari* (date unknown), which relates two instances from the life of Ono Takamura, the hero of the *Konjaku* tale quoted in full above; this work has also been called a diary and even has been referred to as a poetry collection.

We have seen that there is a theory that such works are originally connected with ancient beliefs and the rise of certain families. A good number of the earliest ones, in particular, contain supernatural elements, although this is certainly not always the case. The loss of so many of these works is regrettable, for study of them could probably tell us a great deal about the movement from belief to fiction. The oldest of the extant romances, *Taketori Monogatari* [The Tale of the Bamboo Cutter], has as its main theme the mixing of the mortal and supernatural realms.

Taketori occupies an important position in the history of Japanese literature and there is a variant of it in *Konjaku Monogatari-shū*, so for these reasons I shall spend some time discussing it. Its plot is fairly simple—an old bamboo cutter finds a beautiful young lady about three inches in height in the joint of a bamboo plant and takes her home to care for. She grows larger and more beautiful and the old man becomes wealthy, finding gold inside bamboo shoots frequently. His adopted daughter is besieged by suitors, but refuses to marry. Five of the suitors prove particularly persistent so she assigns impossible tasks to them, promising to marry the man who does what she has required of him.

We then have a short diversion as each suitor attempts unsuccessfully to fulfill his task. One concocts an elaborate scheme to deceive the young lady but is foiled when a craftsman enters the grounds and demands to be paid for having made the jeweled branch the suitor has supposedly just brought from a mythical island; one tells a rather tall tale; still another simply fails, bullied by the dragon from whom he was supposed to bring a jewel; and the final suitor, who has been told to bring the easy birth charm used by a swallow, falls from the tree he has climbed, breaking most of his bones but still clutching to the feces he has grabbed from the nest thinking it was the charm.

Finally the emperor himself comes courting. The lady falls in love with him but explains that it will be impossible for her to marry, as she has come from the moon and is due to return soon. The emperor proves powerless to prevent this and is left with a medicine for long life which the lady gives him. Saying that he will not live forever separated from his beloved, he has the medicine burned on the top of Mt. Fuji (as the highest mountain in Japan, it is the closest to the moon). This, we are told, accounts for the name *Fuji,* which means "not to die."

Without going into any great detail, I will note that there are many stories in Japanese folklore about marriages between mortal men and supernatural women, but that these marriages inevitably fail when the woman is revealed in her true form to the man. The *Taketori* story could be put into this tale cycle without much difficulty.[14] It is not a *setsuwa* in the form it takes in *Taketori Monogatari* because it is too long and is centered around the personality of the woman rather than any particular event. As we shall see, however, it was also told as a *setsuwa.*

According to Mitani Eiichi, at least three of the five suitors were modeled on real, historical people, who were associated with the powerful Fujiwara family. He holds that the contempt with which they are treated shows a discontent with the Fujiwara and that the work becomes more literary through this use of symbolism.[15] However one views this approach to the work, we can say that *Taketori* has applied aristocratic views of beauty to an old story and if only for this reason has considerable claims to being called a work of art. The dominant mood it establishes is one of pathos, the beauty of a failed love. The presence of the suitors tends to make the emperor's acceptance by the woman all the more moving because she tries so hard to keep from becoming involved in a love affair of this world. The accounts of the suitors are amusing and *Taketori* doubtless appealed to both the sense of beauty and the sense of humor of those who read it.

This story is a very popular one and has been told in a number of different contexts.[16] It appears in *Konjaku* XXXI.33 in a form which is considerably different and more typical of the *setsuwa*, and a comparison of the two treatments is instructive.

In the *Konjaku* version, which is much shorter, the old man finds the girl as he has in *Taketori,* brings her home, and grows wealthy. There are suitors but they are not named and we have no narration of their attempts to perform the tasks which are assigned to them, being told only that they all failed and some became Buddhist monks while others went so far as to die of their love. The emperor appears on cue but is more arrogant and not so sensitive as the emperor in *Taketori.*

In the *Konjaku* tale the emperor decides to look at the lady and to take her to the court with him if she is really as beautiful as he has heard; there is no hint of any love between the two. In fact, when the woman says she must return to the sky from whence she came the emperor does not believe her. He makes no attempt to prevent her return to her celestial dwelling as he does in *Taketori.* The compiler of *Konjaku* ends his tale by telling us that no one knows where the woman was from or what she was doing on earth. There is no reference to medicine which will make the emperor live forever and no mention of Mt. Fuji.

In short, the woman has virtually no personality in this version of the tale. All the compiler has found important here is the unique nature of the story. He is not concerned with showing us the poetic nature of the situation or the pathos, only in making the point that sometimes we might encounter beings who are not really of this world. The *Konjaku* story has none of the humor of the older work and very little of its literary merit; it does not go much beyond recording the event as a fact.

If this story was indeed originally associated with the founding of some family, these two versions indicate the different roads the tale travelled: the *Taketori* version is a retelling of the tale as fiction, from the perspective of a poet attempting to present a scene beautiful in its pathos, while the *Konjaku* version is a retelling of the tale as a legend intended to demonstrate to its readers that such events do indeed take place.

This is not to say, of course, that the romances are therefore literature and the *setsuwa* collections are not. It does, however, indicate an obvious difference in the two forms: romances were told primarily for entertainment and the type of entertainment one expected to receive from them was tied up with lyric poetry; *setsuwa*, on the other hand, were told primarily for education and could educate on a wide range of topics. It is when something intervenes to raise the stories above their original purposes of education or entertainment that we begin to speak of them as literature, and this happens throughout much of *Konjaku* and in works like *Taketori*. This "something" is a desire by the compiler, author or poet to go beyond his material, to use his material to probe into the nature of life.

Because the *setsuwa* collections are often educational, they are generally more realistic than are the romances. Even so, stories in the Heian period have close enough ties to *setsuwa* that all have a certain element of realism about them. Even elements of fantasy such as we find in *Taketori* would have been thought plausible by the audience, although I do not mean to suggest that the audience would have believed that the story actually happened. Later works in the romance genre such as *Utsubo Monogatari, Genji Monogatari,* and *Ochikubo Monogatari* begin very much like *Taketori*, with elements of the märchen, but change into more socially realistic stories. This indicates a gradual shifting of the form from supernatural to more worldly concerns. Poetry, in the final analysis, makes the *monogatari* more secular, while also making it more aesthetic.

Summary.   Literature in the Heian period is composed of poetry, poetic diaries, and two different types of prose. One of these is the romance, which is fabricated and told primarily as fiction for entertainment; the second type is the true story, treated more as fact and told primarily for education. This includes such genres as *setsuwa* collections, poem tales, and history tales. It is likely that these two types had a common origin in Japanese myth. The importance of poetry in the development of certain types of prose should not be overlooked, however, for works such as *Ise Monogatari* consist of prose explanations of the poems, and the poetic diary also relies heavily on prose to explain why certain poems were composed. Both the poem tales and the diaries contain and record truth, but present rather subjective renditions of this truth.

There are many poem tales to be found within *setsuwa* collections such as *Konjaku Monogatari-shū* and this is one factor which suggests that *Konjaku* is a truly pivotal work, one which has similarities to both the romance and the other genres of prose. However one may conceive of Heian literature, though, it is difficult to say that *Konjaku* is somehow outside the mainstream, for it simply has too much in common with other genres to allow us to view it in isolation. Let us now proceed to the Kamakura period and consider *Konjaku* against the setting of medieval literature.

Konjaku Monogatari-shū and Medieval Literature

In 1185 Minamoto Yoritomo established a military government in Kamakura, a city near the present Tokyo, and brought the Heian period to a close. This was not something which happened suddenly; it was the culmination of a long series of events. *Konjaku Monogatari-shū* was written toward the close of the Heian period, and many scholars have hailed it as the first work to celebrate the new medieval consciousness.[17] Because *Konjaku* was written in a period of transformation it is not surprising that such opinions have appeared. In Chapter 1 I argued that the Buddhism found in *Konjaku* has closer ties to the so-called "old" Heian Buddhism than it does to the "new" Kamakura sects; what, then is the situation in respect to the Heian and medieval literary genres?

The main genre of literature in the Kamakura period—leaving aside for the moment the *setsuwa* collections, which by bulk alone should be considered the most popular form of literature during that era—is the war tale (*gunki*). The most important of these is *Heike Monogatari,* which has a complex textual history but appears to be a combination of both written and chanted versions and to have been put together in its present form in the mid-thirteenth century.[18] Other important works are *Heiji Monogatari* (around 1220), *Hōgen Monogatari* (about the same time), and *Taiheiki* (probably completed around 1370). The genres important in the Heian period—specifically, the diary and the romance—continued to be produced, but on a much smaller scale, and are not particularly important.

In addition to being characterized as the literature of the warrior Kamakura literature is also sometimes called the literature of the hermit. Works like *Hōjōki* (1212), by the hermit Kamo no Chōmei, were also popular, and there was a general tendency on the part of aristocrats to renounce the world for the religious life. Poetry became more introspective and personal, moving beyond the "elegant confusion" found so frequently in the Heian collections to works which celebrate emptiness and loneliness. The thirty-one-syllable *tanka*, however, continued to be the major verse form.

Another important product of the Kamakura period is the Nō drama. The Nō is characterized by having little action, most of its meaning being couched in symbolism. It was strongly associated with warriors and is also often associated with the doctrines of Zen Buddhism.

Later in the Kamakura period we move to a government by the military class with the emperor and court nobles very much in the background, both politically and economically. The lyric becomes more personal and introspective and in the field of prose fiction we find that war tales glorifying the deeds of soldiers have become popular. In this section I will examine *Konjaku* in terms of the war tales and also in terms of a later medieval genre of popular literature known as *otogizōshi*, which was popular in the Muromachi period (1333–1600) and later.

War Tales.   The most important war tale is the lengthy *Heike Monogatari* [Tales of the Heike]. This work was probably completed in its present form in the mid-thirteenth century; its material is the series of wars between the Taira family (also known as the Heike) and the Minamoto family (also known as the Genji). The Minamoto were the final victors with Minamoto Yoritomo becoming the first military ruler of Japan, but the Taira are the clear victors in a literary sense and it is after them that the book is named.

The Taira family came to prominence in 1156, when Taira Kiyomori arrived in the capital after having defeated the Genji in a succession dispute called the Hōgen disturbance (itself the inspiration for an earlier war tale, *Hōgen Monogatari*); until 1179 Kiyomori actually shared power with the retired Emperor Go-Shirakawa. The clan lost all power when it was completely defeated by a rejuvenated Genji clan in 1183. The main reason for the defeat of the Heike is that Kiyomori attempted to control the country in the traditional manner—from the capital, with no system of dependent vassals in the provinces.

Because its methods were similar to those used by the aristocratic families earlier in the Heian period, the public image of the Heike gradually changed from a level slightly above that of the lowest barbarians to one almost equal to that of the cultured aristocrats. The defeat of the Heike was seen as the defeat of the old order and there was a good deal of sympathy for them among the aristocrats. Kiyomori in particular is held up in *Heike* as an example of how the powerful in this world are always doomed to ruin. The most popular of the Minamoto was Yoritomo's younger half-brother Yoshitsune, who was put to death by Yoritomo.

Hence the work is called the tales of the *Heike,* and the sympathies of the readers were with that clan rather than with the victorious Genji. *Heike Monogatari* is permeated with the idea of *mujō,* or a sense of impermanence, which is the aesthetic glue holding the work together, keeping it from becoming a mere succession of battle stories and exploits of the members of the two main families. As is so often the case in Japanese literature, beauty here is found in weakness and defeat.

The texts of this work are numerous and the study of the textual history of *Heike* is a field of academic endeavor in itself. Basically there are two types of texts, those which were written and those which were chanted. The chanted texts (*yomi-hon*) were probably prepared by blind, lute-playing Buddhist monks (*biwa hōshi*) who made their livings by traveling through the country reciting the stories from the *Heike* cycle. The present text used by most editions of the work is thought to have been put together from both the written and chanted texts by Buddhist monks.

We can see, then, that there are certain similarities between a collection of *setsuwa* such as *Konjaku Monogatari-shū* and war tales such as *Heike Monogatari*. Both works are made up of short episodes and have been put together by Buddhists involved in preaching, both are organized and unified by Buddhist thought prominent at the time. *Heike,* of course, is a much more unified work, with its episodes forming one complete story, unlike the tales of *Konjaku,* and there is an obvious danger in attempting to push the analogy too far. One should not, however, lose sight of the fact that the majority of the individual episodes in *Heike* could be told independently of the work as a whole and if they were they would resemble nothing more than *setsuwa* of the sort found in *Konjaku.*

This similarity in form is not, however, the main basis for the claim that *Konjaku* somehow represents a new, medieval consciousness; rather, the claim is made on the basis of the fact that *Konjaku* XXV contains fourteen war tales. Because there are war tales in *Konjaku,* and because war tales were so important in medieval Japanese literature, the argument goes, *Konjaku* really should be considered as a medieval work. Although *Konjaku* also contains an entire volume and more of poem tales, incidentally, it is not argued on this basis that it is really an aristocratic work.

To understand what distinguishes *Konjaku* from medieval Japanese literature we must consider the differences between scene and mood. The *Konjaku* compiler painted a fairly accurate picture of his world, certainly more so than did the writers of the Heian romances. Characters of all sorts fill his pages, warriors and peasants as well as aristocrats. This sweeping picture of all of the layers of his society is what distinguishes the *Konjaku* compiler's *scenes* from those of the romances and diaries.

Konjaku's mood, however, seems to be predominantly Heian. It would be a mistake to assume that simply because he describes warriors in his stories the *Konjaku* compiler actually liked these people. A careful reading of the war tales will reveal a basic lack of sympathy for the warrior.

To illustrate, I will compare descriptions of the deaths of two warriors—Taira Masakado and Kiso Yoshinaka—as found in *Konjaku* and *Heike,* respectively. Both of these men were considered enemies of the state and both suffered ignoble deaths. First, *Konjaku* on Masakado:[19]

Masakado spurred on his horse and entered the battle personally. There must have been divine retribution, for his horse would not gallop and his aim was not good. Finally he was hit by an arrow and died in the field. The opposing generals rejoiced and dispatched a fierce warrior to take his head.

Now, *Heike* on Yoshinaka. Yoshinaka had been aligned with Yoritomo, but attempted to form his own revolt and was thus attacked by Yoritomo's forces. In this scene Yoshinaka's force has been reduced to himself and his loyal retainer Imai Kanehira; Imai has urged Yoshinaka to commit suicide rather than be cut down by an unworthy foe, and is struggling with the enemy to allow Yoshinaka time for a proper suicide:

It was toward dusk on the twenty-first day of the first month; thin ice was everywhere. He could not tell marsh from field, and though he urged his horse on it sank to its neck in the mud. He spurred it on and spurred it on, and whipped it and whipped it, but it would not move. Thinking of the sad plight of Imai, he turned to look. A retainer of Ishida, one Tamehisa, hit him under his helmet with an arrow. . . . Two of Ishida's men then fell on Yoshinaka and cut off his head.

Clearly the author of *Heike* feels sympathy even for a traitor such as Yoshinaka, and describes his death in a way calculated to move his readers to sympathy. The death of Masakado, on the other hand, has the same potential for pathos but is described in *Konjaku* by an unsympathetic compiler and thus does not move us. This is made even more noticeable by the fact that the *Heike* author felt sympathy for Masakado and used him as an example when listing the names of some of those in history who attained great heights only to lose their power and die lonely deaths.

There are other examples in the *Konjaku* war tales of this basic unsympathetic attitude toward the warriors. In XXV.3, for example, we have the story of two warriors who decide to reduce a large-scale battle to a personal contest so that lives will not be wasted; when neither proves a winner they call the whole thing off. The *Konjaku* compiler says approvingly, "Warriors of antiquity were such people." The implication is clear as regards the warriors of present times.

A search through the *Konjaku* war tales will not turn up a single instance of the use of the word *mujō* ("impermanence") which is so important in *Heike*. We find one instance of the use of *aware* ("pathetic"), a word which is used often to describe the waning beauty of an aristocratic woman and which had positive connotations to the *Konjaku* compiler. This case is XXV.4, a story about a young aristocrat who slips into the tent of the warrior who killed his father and kills the warrior in his sleep. This is seen as a moving act by the compiler although it would have been thought despicable by any warrior because it violates the code of bravery.

In short, even though there are tales about warriors in *Konjaku Monogatari-shū*, there is no evidence to suggest that the compiler has included them out of any great sympathy or respect for the class as a whole. We should not let their presence in the collection lead us to believe that the compiler was embracing the new world order; although his view of society is considerably wider than most Heian works his sympathies were not. It can be argued that there are similarities of form between *setsuwa* and war tales, and even that some of the later *setsuwa* collections have close connections to the war tales and to medieval literature in general, but *Konjaku Monogatari-shū* remains essentially a product of the Heian period.

Other Medieval Genres.   I will not discuss drama in any detail here, noting only that several of the *Konjaku* stories have also been treated by the Nō playwrights. In fact, the legend is one of the chief building blocks of Nō, although the Nō treatment of the stories has very little in common with the treatment one finds in *setsuwa* collections. *Setsuwa* were important to writers of the Nō for two basic reasons—the audience was already familiar with the stories, and the stories have a close connection to living folk belief, particularly belief connected with the supernatural, something which was used by Nō playwrights in their efforts to explore man's place in the world.

A somewhat later genre with close ties to *setsuwa* literature is the Muromachi short story, commonly referred to as *otogi-zōshi* ("notebooks for companions"). This name presents a problem to the scholar for it was first used to describe only one type of format found in Muromachi literature, only later being adopted as the name of a genre. It has come to have connotations similar to the English "nursery story," and the name should be abandoned. For many years the genre was considered as being fit only for women, children, and other semiliterates; only recently has it been receiving the scholarly attention it deserves.

The typical Muromachi short story is longer than the average *setsuwa,* running to as many as twenty pages on occasion. It differs from *setsuwa* in other ways as well. Primary among these is the fact that the stories are generally hero-centered rather than event-centered. Ichiko Teiji has divided the tales into six general categories, based on their subject matter. These are stories about aristocrats, religious tales, warrior tales, stories about commoners, stories which take place in real or fictional foreign lands, and stories about nonhumans.[20] The stories were apparently told mostly by word of mouth, by traveling Buddhist monks and nuns, generally to crowds in the marketplaces in cities.

As an example of stories in this genre I will briefly discuss a tale called "Monokusa Tarō" [The Lazy Youth]. The hero of this story is extremely lazy, eating only when he is given food. One day he has an encounter with the governor of his province and as a result of this the governor decides he really is hopeless and commands the farmers in the province to support the youth. Later the province is asked to supply a long-term servant to the capital; seeing their chance to rid themselves of this nuisance the farmers send Monokusa Tarō. When he arrives at the capital his personality apparently undergoes a dramatic change, for he becomes industrious.

He courts and wins a woman by demonstrating a remarkable skill in poetry and word games which overcomes her initial disgust with him. She cleans him up and finally he is introduced to the emperor himself, whom he impresses by making a good poem. The hero is awarded the governorship of two provinces after the emperor discovers that he is a descendant of the imperial family. We are then told that he was the earthly incarnation of a deity.

This tale has few if any surface connections with *setsuwa* literature. It is fairly long and definitely hero-centered; further, it seems to have been told for the entertainment of the common people rather than for an aristocratic audience. It has but scant connection to Buddhism even though it does contain religious motifs and was probably influenced by Buddhist thought. It was, however, based on oral tradition and has many parallels in Japanese folk tales.

The story of Monokusa Tarō was thought to have great power for those who heard it, and the narrator assures us at the end of the story that those who hear it every day will certainly grow wealthy. It will be remembered that the compilers of some *setsuwa* collections undertook their tasks because they believed that they would achieve salvation if they were associated with the holy stories they were telling.

One big difference between the *setsuwa* and Muromachi short stories is the method of transmission in each case. Many of the Muromachi tales were the product of oral tradition and many were performed; the act of performance is important in a consideration of their structures. The use of pictures was important in the performance, as was the use of music. It is doubtful that *setsuwa* were often performed in such a way, for the telling of a *setsuwa* generally came as a part of some larger event such as a religious ceremony. The Muromachi stories were enjoyed at least in part because they were performed; their form was fixed and stories were associated with professional entertainers. In the case of the *setsuwa* the content of the story is more important than its form and the story might be told by a variety of narrators for a variety of reasons.

The stories of the Muromachi period were recited or performed by professionals to an audience of nonprofessionals. In the case of most of the genres of the Heian period we have no such distinction between artist and audience; nearly all of the Heian aristocrats were, for example, both writers and readers of poetry. Those who wrote obviously had similar concerns with those who read. This increase in distance between writer and reader is of great importance in the development of literature in the Muromachi period. It has its beginnings with war tales such as *Heike Monogatari,* which was also recited by a professional class of blind lute players.

Even within the tradition of Heian literature, however, we can find some distance between producer and consumer if we consider the case of *setsuwa* literature. Some of the preaching monks fill the role of performer, and in the case of a monk preaching to an audience there must have been some distance between audience and writer. Indeed, the performing arts and performance literature of the Muromachi and Edo periods might well be traced back to works such as *Konjaku,* which was among the first to make use of a more public approach to literature. There has been little research done on this topic but it does seem that *Konjaku Monogatari-shū* has some importance within the overall history of performance literature in Japan.

Konjaku Monogatari-shū in Modern Japanese Literature

It is not surprising that a collection such as *Konjaku* should have been noticed and appreciated by modern writers. It offers a sweeping view of society and a series of unusual and dramatically narrated stories with heroes who are in some ways more real than those of the court romances such as *Genji Monogatari.* There are several modern writers who have made use of material from *Konjaku* but I will deal briefly here only with the best known of these, the short-story writer Akutagawa Ryūnosuke (1892–1927).

Although it is not often acknowledged in Western studies of his work, most of Akutagawa's best-known works were adaptations from either *Konjaku* or *Uji Shūi Monogatari.* A look at his views on the subject and his treatments of the stories will reveal much about *Konjaku,* for Akutagawa was a most perceptive critic.

In a penetrating essay Akutagawa says he was drawn to *Konjaku* and other *setsuwa* collections because of their "primitive beauty." He says that "freshness" could be called "the artistic life of *Konjaku Monogatari,*"[21] seeing in the stories in the collection a true human comedy which depicts people as they really are. He held that the "primitive" nature of *Konjaku* is an effective contrast to more aesthetic works such as *Genji* and he was much impressed with the raw power of many of the *Konjaku* narratives. Akutagawa preferred the Japanese secular stories to the Buddhist tales but he also admired the Buddhist tales, and even writes admiringly of the stories in the Indian volumes.

Akutagawa was most impressed by the realistic nature of the *Konjaku* narrative style. He says that because the compiler did not add to or detract from reality he was in effect writing a type of psychological fiction. It was this quality which Akutagawa attempted to expand in his own works based on *Konjaku* stories.

At the time Akutagawa was writing, the most important type of fiction being produced in Japan was the so-called "I-novel," a confessional type of novel based on the life of the writer. Akutagawa apparently felt that such novels were of no particular use because the novelist was too close to his material to present it in a psychologically realistic manner. In his own works he creates considerably more distance between characters and writer than was common during his day, looking closely at the motives behind the characters' actions.

The best known of Akutagawa's *Konjaku* derivations is a story called "In a Grove," adapted from *Konjaku* XXIX.23. The tale in *Konjaku* relates how a thief lures a traveler and his wife into a grove, ties up the man, and rapes the wife. Akutagawa's version of this tale inspired the movie *Rashōmon,* directed by Kurosawa Akira; in Akutagawa's hands the story becomes a probing into the nature of violence and guilt.

The *Konjaku* tale is short and to the point. The husband is only tied up and forced to watch the rape of his wife, and the compiler even goes so far as to praise the thief for not stealing the woman's clothing. He also says that the husband was stupid for entering the grove with a man he has known for only a day. There is no mention of what happened to the couple or the robber afterwards.

Akutagawa's narrative is considerably different from that of the *Konjaku* compiler. Akutagawa tells the story through a series of testimonies of witnesses, ranging from the magistrate who captured the thief to the stories of the three principle characters. In Akutagawa's tale, however, the husband is murdered after the rape, and a central question posed by the story is that of who the murderer was. The thief confesses the crime in his testimony, but the wife then turns herself over to the authorities and makes her own confession. Finally the murdered man is contacted through a medium and he, too, confesses, saying that he has committed suicide.

Each of the characters tells the tale in a way which makes his or her own role seem the most admirable: the thief depicts himself as a valiant fighter, the wife as a woman who cannot live with her shame, and the husband as a wronged innocent who has been humiliated by both thief and wife (the wife, in his version, offers to run away with the thief). The reader is left to come to her own understanding of truth.

In his film treatment of the story Kurosawa also uses this narrative style and for good measure throws in a final witness, a woodcutter who has supposedly seen the incident and who can thus provide us with a more objective view. In both Akutagawa's story and the film the implication is that truth is subjective and that we will never know who the murderer was.

Akutagawa has taken considerable liberties with the story here and with most of the other stories he has adapted as well. This is in complete keeping with the more traditional role of the transmitter of a *setsuwa,* for as we have seen, compilers were perfectly willing to make whatever changes in the story material their editorial plans or purposes called for. Akutagawa's view that truth is subjective and impossible to determine is, further, in general agreement with the views of the *Konjaku* compiler on the subject of reality and illusion.

What attracted Akutagawa to this and other stories was the unusual nature of the story itself. Once more we see the power of the *setsuwa* to communicate, for this has always been the reason *setsuwa* were born. This attraction points to an important feature of *Konjaku Monogatari-shū* which I would like to stress once again—the tales in *Konjaku* are dramatically narrated and many of them have exerted considerable power on their readers.

The core story in any given *setsuwa,* then, is seldom altered, no matter how many incarnations the story may go through or how many different morals are added by different collectors. Although Akutagawa, for example, never uses the morals added to the stories by the *Konjaku* compiler, he does not change the basic core of the tale—any changes he makes are a matter of reinterpretation of the material from his own perspective. The perspectives held by Akutagawa and the *Konjaku* compiler generally differ but the stories themselves act as powerful magnets.

It would be impossible to discuss in any detail all of the tales Akutagawa has adapted from *Konjaku* or *Uji Shūi*. A partial list of some of the best known would include "Rashōmon," "Yam Gruel," "The Nose," "The Dragon," "Hell Screen," "A Picture Scroll of Salvation," "The Princess of the Sixth Ward," "The Robbers," and more. We can note that he consistently reinterprets the tales and is especially interested in what motivates the characters.

The distance Akutagawa is able to gain from his characters by using familiar stories is one not achieved by I-novelists who were contemporary with him, who tended to identify almost completely with their characters. This same type of distance is ultimately one of the main factors which distinguishes *Konjaku* from the more lyrical works of the Heian period. In examining the overwhelmingly lyrical literary tradition of Japan with all its emphasis on the exploration of the internal world of the artist, it is important to remember that works such as *Konjaku Monogatari-shū* and writers like Akutagawa also found room to exist.

Conclusion

Konjaku Monogatari-shū is truly a pivotal work that stands partially within two distinct traditions in the history of Japanese literature. The first of these is the lyrical tradition of the Heian period, for even though the form of *Konjaku* is prose, many of its methods are lyrical. The compiler makes great use of lyrical devices such as association, juxtaposition, and the development of theme in a suggestive manner; he seems to have learned much of this from the poetic practices of his day. In addition to these lyrical qualities *Konjaku* shares with other Heian literature a worldview that is essentially world affirming. Although the *Konjaku* compiler recognizes that there is much in the present world which is not good and should be changed, he does not look back to the past for his escape nor does he attempt to hide himself from the troubles of the present through a retreat into introspection. He rather faces the world squarely and offers his readers a set of blueprints they can use for success in their present situation. His approach to the world, if not his proposed method of coping with it, is hence very much in line with the traditional Heian approach.

In this sense *Konjaku* is clearly a product of the Heian tradition. The medieval approach to the times was most generally one which denied the world and attempted to find solace elsewhere. Even a work such as *Heike Monogatari* is permeated with the idea of *mujō* ("impermanence") and celebrates the loser and the glories of a time now past. When the Heian poet looked on a cherry tree in full bloom he celebrated the beauty of the flowers knowing full well that they were soon to disappear, and this worship of frail beauty we now call *aware;* the medieval poet was more apt to celebrate the beauty of the flowers after they had fallen, finding great significance in the fact that they once were beautiful and were now gone. The *Konjaku* compiler might be said to have been watching the flowers as they swirled to the ground, giving them advice as to how to land softly and avoid injury.

But we also have in the medieval period the flourishing of a different type of literature, a literature which was chanted or read aloud and intended for a broader audience than was the literature of the Heian period. The war tales were chanted by blind lute-playing Buddhist monks and in the Muromachi period we find a full-blown genre of performed literature. If one defines "medieval" in these terms, there is indeed much in *Konjaku* that is medieval, for it certainly was used by preachers and many of its stories are drawn from oral tradition.

Further, *Konjaku* offers a contrast to Heian literature in its narrative style and its descriptions of an external world rather than an internal one. In this aspect it represents a different type of development of story than was common in the Heian romance. The romance was appreciated more for its form, which was influenced by poetic convention, while the more factual stories in *Konjaku* were appreciated for content and the interest inherent in the unusual nature of the stories they related. It was this aspect of *setsuwa* literature that attracted modern writers such as Akutagawa Ryūnosuke.

Let us turn, finally, to an assessment of those factors which the *Konjaku* compiler used to transform individual *setsuwa* into works which we today would call literature.

Chapter Five
A Critical Overview

It is difficult, if not impossible, to assign a work like *Konjaku Monogatari-shū* to its "proper place" in the history of Japanese literature, for the collection is simply too vast and complex to fit into any neatly pigeonholed scheme. *Konjaku* has often been considered as somehow less than literature, as an artless collection of tales which is of value primarily because it can give us a more complete picture of the times during which it was produced. Few would persist in this view now, although critical examinations into its literary nature have taken the back seat in deference to more technical studies concerning the relationships between texts and the like.

There is still a decided trend among scholars in the West to ignore *setsuwa* collections when speaking of Japanese literary history; Heian literature continues to be defined in terms of the lyrical genres such as the poetic diaries and the romances.

But if *Konjaku Monogatari-shū* is not a *Genji Monogatari* it nonetheless has many things which *Genji* lacks. Certainly one would not call *Genji* inferior because it does not have the narrative style of *Konjaku,* and it seems just as simplistic to say that *Konjaku* is lacking because it does not have *Genji*'s lyrical intensity or memorable portraits of court ladies.

When considering the literary nature of *Konjaku,* then, we should concentrate on those factors which are unique to it in the history of Japanese literature and avoid judging it against other completely different works. What is it that makes *Konjaku* unique, both within the *setsuwa* genre and Japanese literature as a whole?

An answer to this question requires a brief recapitulation of some of the basic information about the collection. *Konjaku* is composed of *setsuwa,* which are short tales about some event that is out of the ordinary. This extraordinary aspect of the individual stories is what provides them with their initial interest and is why they have been orally transmitted and then taken over by the compilers of the *setsuwa* collections.

The extraordinary nature *of* the tale, however, is only one aspect of a collection such as *Konjaku. Konjaku* is a collection intended for the education and religious salvation of its readers, and each story included in the collection contributes in some way to that goal. Hence, the interest the compiler feels *in* his stories may not be exactly the same as the interest *of* the story as it was originally told or as it was in the form that the compiler first saw it. In short, *Konjaku Monogatari-shū* is a collection, with internal unity and wholeness; in addition to considering the nature of any particular story on its own we must also consider it as a unit in the collection as a whole.

In order to approach *Konjaku* as a work of literature, I will examine first its narrative style, to see how the compiler handles his individual building blocks, the *setsuwa* which make up his collection. Then I will consider some ways in which the individual tales fit together within the collection, losing their individual identity as the compiler uses them to make suggestions about some higher truth than might be seen in a story-by-story examination of the tales as individual units. In both sections we must be aware of the fact that the compiler's individual vision of the world has worked to reshape the stories he includes in his collection.

Before proceeding, then, let me briefly reiterate the essentials of the compiler's vision. The compiler was living in a world fraught with social and cultural changes, changes which were not to the advantage of the traditional aristocratic classes. In Buddhist terms, too, the world was less than desirable, for the period of the latter days of the law (*mappō*) had begun and it was impossible for an individual to gain salvation on his own merits. To cope with this world the compiler urged cleverness and faith, the faith being in some powerful symbol of Buddhism such as the Lotus Sutra or the Western Paradise of Amida. The idea of faith and the belief that an individual could not by himself distinguish truth from falsehood can be seen in one way or another in nearly all of the stories in the Japanese section—both Buddhist and secular—in the collection.

Konjaku Monogatari-shū: The Nature of Its Narrative

As a rule, *Konjaku* stories are fairly specific as to time, place and person. In this regard we might note that the collection contains several lacunae in places where such information is called for, which indicates that the compiler did not have the appropriate information at his fingertips and intended to do some further research and add it at a later date, then was unable to do so for one reason or another.[1]

In addition, *Konjaku* descriptions pay a great deal of attention to external details such as articles of clothing and the like. There is little description of the psychology of the characters or their innermost feelings, although their thoughts are often reported as quotations. The narrative is usually rather sparse, containing few digressions from the general story line, although it may contain details which could be omitted.

Konjaku narratives are also often dramatic, with a fairly liberal use of dialogue or monologue to make the action of the story more immediate. The compiler seldom addresses the reader directly, except for the morals or conclusions he inevitably appends to his stories. In these cases he changes his role from narrator to commentator for the occasion.

In order to understand more specifically how the *Konjaku* compiler works to make his treatments of stories immediate and dramatic to his audience, I will compare his treatments to those of other compilers, looking at what the *Konjaku* compiler has added to the tales. One could find literally hundreds of examples to work from, and I will confine myself to only two, one having a Chinese and the other a Japanese source. We have seen in Chapter 2 some other examples of differences in treatment between *Konjaku* and works like *Uji Shūi Monogatari, Kohon Setsuwa-shū, Uchigiki-shū,* and the like.

Konjaku VI.11, it will be remembered, is the story of how an evil man in China is saved from death because he once gave some money to his brother to assist him in the commissioning of a portrait of Buddha. The hero of the story actually dies and goes to the underworld, and is saved there and brought back to life. The source for this story is the Chinese collection *San-pao Kan-ying Yao-lüeh Lu,* and the *Konjaku* version makes but few changes in this Chinese source. Those changes that are made, however, are worth noting.

In the Chinese version of the tale the hero dies as a result of a fall from his horse while hunting. The story reads simply, "He went out for a hunt and fell from his horse." The *Konjaku* compiler, however, has this section read, "He went out to the mountain fields to hunt and just as he was about to shoot a deer he unexpectedly fell from his horse." The statement of fact in the source conveys the situation, but not in a very interesting or even realistic manner, while the *Konjaku* compiler makes the story more immediately interesting by locating the action more precisely.

When the hero of this story is revived, he relates how he was taken to the court of the dead; he simply says that he was put in a cart and taken away, but in *Konjaku* the compiler has added the phrase, "as I was wondering what kind of cart this could be." This also makes the story more appealing because it capitalizes on the extraordinary and unworldly nature of the experience of the hero.

The *Konjaku* compiler also recreates situations more realistically; after the hero falls from his horse and dies he adds the following sentence, not found in his source: "The retainers all gathered around moaning." It is probable that this would happen, and little details like this one and those mentioned above work to make the story more immediate and realistic to the reader.

The above is a case of relatively minor changes which work to make the *Konjaku* treatment more realistic and vivid, but the *Konjaku* compiler sometimes made wholesale changes in his material in order to have the story conform to his editorial plan as well as to his narrative style. A good case in point here is a rather wholesale reworking of a tale from *Nihon Ryōiki* (I.7), a story about a monk whose boat is attacked by pirates and who is then saved by a turtle he has earlier bought from a fisherman and released into the sea. The *Konjaku* adaptation of the story is XIX.30.

The *Konjaku* compiler begins his rewriting of this story from the very beginning of the tale. The *Ryōiki* version begins by naming the hero of the story, a Korean-born monk named Gusai, then briefly relates how Gusai happened to come to Japan. The story of the monk's arrival in Japan is built around the tale of a Japanese official who had gone to Korea and was unable to return home due to political unrest; he finally made a vow to Buddha to dedicate a temple if he was allowed free passage home. This was then granted him, and he brought the monk with him in order to better carry out his vow. Gusai's trip to the capital was on business pertaining to the fulfilling of the vow.

In the *Konjaku* version, however, we do not see Gusai at the beginning of the tale. Rather, the compiler has begun by giving us the story about the Japanese official, and only later does he introduce Gusai. This device gives Gusai's trip to the capital more dramatic significance, because we have been shown rather than told its significance.

Such a difference in approach is appropriate in *Konjaku* for another reason as well—although the *Ryōiki* tale is really centered around the nobility of the turtle which repaid its debt of gratitude by saving the monk, the *Konjaku* version centers on the ideas of holiness and compassion and the results of these virtues. By introducing Gusai only after the nature of his mission to the capital has been explained the *Konjaku* compiler is able to show us more convincingly the aura of holiness that surrounds him. In this way the compiler shifts the tale from one urging that human beings should follow the example of this turtle and always repay their debts of gratitude to one about the rewards for compassion shown to a holy person.

A glance at the endings of the stories will confirm this observation. The *Ryōiki* tale ends with the following exhortation:

Even beasts, then, do not forget debts of gratitude, but always repay them. How, we must ask, could a man of virtue ever possibly forget such a debt?

Konjaku, on the other hand, omits this exhortation and merely notes:

This is not the first incident of a turtle paying back a debt of gratitude to a man. It is said such things began in India and China and finally spread to this country.

Thus the *Konjaku* compiler changes the emphasis of the tale, moving it from a simple didactic message about the importance of repaying debts of gratitude to a slightly more complex story about the benefits of holiness and compassion.

This is not, however, the only type of change the compiler has made in the story. He also makes changes in the narrative to conform to his general dramatic style of storytelling. As an example, consider the point in the story when Gusai is forced to jump overboard from his boat by the pirates and is then saved by the turtle. In the *Ryōiki* version this is described in the following way:

When he had reached water to his waist his feet struck a rock; when he looked the next morning he found that it was a turtle's shell. He was in the harbor of Binchū, and the turtle bowed its head three times and swam away. He wondered if this could have been the turtle he had set free, now repaying its debt of gratitude.

Now the *Konjaku* version:

Gusai jumped into the ocean and when he did he sank into the water up to about his waist, then his feet hit something like a rock. He stood there in the sea like that all night, and at dawn he saw that he was standing on the shell of a large turtle. When he looked around he found himself in the inlet near Bingo.

His surprise at seeing this was boundless. At dusk he had met with pirates near Honejima in Bizen and now he looked around and saw that he was in the inlet near Bingo. In one night he had come through two provinces. "How long would it take to get here?" he wondered, and his surprise was boundless.

He went ashore from there and thought, "The turtle which I bought and let go into the ocean yesterday must have saved me to repay its debt." He thought this was indeed touching and holy.

It is obvious that the *Konjaku* compiler has greatly embellished this episode.

The story in *Ryōiki* is not without dramatic interest, but there is no comparison with the *Konjaku* tale. The *Konjaku* uses internal monologue to make the action more immediate; instead of being told about the man's surprise or his speculation about the turtle we have been shown them, which is a more effective way to tell the story. This makes the story more immediate to the reader than it was in the source.

In addition to using a more immediate narrative style the *Konjaku* compiler puts added emphasis on the wondrous aspect of the tale, the turtle's speed. The *Konjaku* story has the turtle taking the monk as far as Bingo, which is one province farther than Binchū, where the trip ends for the monk in *Ryōiki*. This added detail and the hero's surprise would have made the story more exciting and it also would have stressed the extraordinary nature of the event.

Kyōkai, the compiler of *Nihon Ryōiki,* sees the tale in terms of its message about repaying debts of gratitude; one might speculate that had he made the events of the story too wondrous he would have weakened his didactic message. Since the *Konjaku* version centers more on the idea of the reward for compassion, it is only natural that the compiler should have made the story as miraculous as possible, for this increases the size of the reward.

The *Konjaku* compiler added another passage to the tale which is not in *Ryōiki* but which is worth considering:

The master of the house listened to the story and said, "To meet with pirates and have all one's property stolen is a common enough thing. The power which saved your life, however, was wholly the turtle's debt of gratitude." He was happy and thought it holy.

We have already seen that *Konjaku* was written during a time of social upheaval and *Ryōiki* was not, so it is not surprising that the compiler should comment on the frequency with which one might be robbed. This addition gives his tale an added dimension, however, for it offers us a way of coping with the evil condition of the world; this solution is compassion such as is expressed by the monk. Compassion, the compiler is telling us, will be repaid in kind, and in these troubled times one needs all the help he can get. To be sure, the *Ryōiki* tale implies that this is the case, but the *Konjaku* compiler is more direct.

This story, in its *Ryōiki* version, is one of several tales about animals (and particularly turtles) repaying debts of gratitude; it ends with an exhortation that humans should do likewise. It has no particular context within the collection, however, and goes no further than conveying this rather simple message.

In the hands of the *Konjaku* compiler, however, the emphasis is shifted. The story becomes an exhortation for humans to show compassion by dramatizing the probable results for those who are compassionate. This type of compassion is associated here with holiness, but more importantly, it is depicted as an asset which will help one make his way through the troubled world. In this respect it is important to note that the hero Gusai at the end of the story recognizes the thieves who have robbed him but says nothing, once more showing the compassion for which he is noted. These changes are consistent with the *Konjaku* compiler's practice of using his tales to demonstrate some larger truth.

The *Konjaku* narrative style, then, is immediate and dramatic, and the compiler consistently works to change his tales so that they will fit his overall concepts of truth as well as conform to his standards of narration. There is one more point that should be made about his narrative style, and that is that it is often quite vivid, sometimes almost to the point of nausea. Consider the following:

After this, although the husband wanted to be with her forever, he had little choice but to put her in a coffin. The day for the funeral was rather distant so he had her in the house for over ten days. The husband felt a limitless love for his dead wife and this love was difficult to endure. Therefore, he opened the coffin to peek in.

Her long hair had come loose and fallen down over the pillow, and her eyes, which had been so charming, had fallen out, leaving a place something like the scar which is left on a tree when a knot has been dug out of it. Her body had turned to a yellowish color and was quite frightening. The bridge of her nose had caved in, causing her nostrils to flare out. Because her lips had wrinkled up like thin paper her upper and lower teeth seemed to be biting sharply into one another. When he looked at that face he felt both disgust and fear and covered it up, fleeing the room. The odor entered his mouth and nose and the stench was without limit; he felt as though he had a lump in his throat.

After this experience, the hero of this tale—XIX.10—decides to become a Buddhist monk.

This vivid sort of narrative is quite effective within the context of *Konjaku Monogatari-shū*'s didactic tales, because it demonstrates the hero's motives in a quite realistic fashion. Such passages as the one quoted above are not placed randomly within the collection, but rather are utilized by the compiler only when it is important that the motives of a particular person be made crystal clear. I would go so far as to say that no other *setsuwa* collection extant uses passages of quite so graphic a nature.

In summary, the *Konjaku* compiler expends a good deal of his narrative skill bringing the situations he describes alive to the reader; these situations are more important to him than the characters who populate his tales. Rather than attempt to understand the characters themselves, he strives to understand those situations which trigger actions, and the result of this is often a vivid and immediate narrative style. The reader is always put close to the action in a *Konjaku* story and seldom is told something that could be shown.

Unusual or out-of-the-ordinary situations provide the initial interest of the stories related in *Konjaku* but the compiler's concerns go beyond the mere reporting of these situations. His major concern is to use the stories he narrates so as to make a larger point. Now let us see how he arranges the tales as building blocks in his efforts to build a collection with some internal unity.

Stories Transformed: From *Setsuwa* to Literature

A *setsuwa* by itself is a thing without fixed form and hence has no claim to any intrinsic literary merit. It is the act of transmission in a collection that sometimes pushes the individual tale from its preliterary state to something which could more accurately be termed literature, and it is therefore the factors leading to this transformation that we must study if we are to understand how the stories in *Konjaku Monogatari-shū* exist as works of literature.

These factors are complex and may best be understood through specific examples. I shall therefore present two tales in complete translation and demonstrate through a discussion of these stories the process by which the *Konjaku* compiler's vision of the world interacts with his material to create something entirely new, a unique work of literature which differs from any other treatment of the same two tales. Before presenting the translations it is necessary to mention that the elements which make up the *Konjaku* literary formula are the tales themselves, the compiler's Buddhist world view, and the compiler's editorial technique. This editorial technique, it will be remembered, has been called *ni wa, ich rui* ("two tales, one type"), and is the method by which the compiler achieved progression and integration of the tales in each individual volume of his collection. The stories in question have been taken from volume XIX, where they are tales 19 and 20.

19:A Tōdai-ji Monk Meets a Dead Monk in the Mountains. Long ago, there was a certain monk who served at the temple Tōdai-ji. Once when he went out to gather flowers in the Eastern mountains he missed his road and became lost in the mountains. Not knowing where he was, he walked along a valley as though in a dream, wondering, "What will happen to me? People who have met with the deity of confusion wander like this. Where am I headed? It all seems so strange!"

While wandering about with such thoughts he came to a place which looked like a long corridor with a tiled roof. He saw some areas which seemed to be individual separated cells like monks' rooms. Fearfully, he entered one of these rooms, to encounter a

monk who had died at Tōdai-ji. When he saw this man his fear
was boundless.

"Surely this monk has become an evil spirit and is living here,"
he thought, but the dead man looked at him and said, "Why
have you come here? This is not a place easily reached by humans.
This is a rare thing indeed."

The living monk replied, "I went up in the mountains to
gather flowers but there were no road marks so I lost my way.
I was wandering around vacantly when I arrived here."

The dead monk said, "This meeting is a very happy thing."
His weeping was without end. The living monk was frightened,
but moved by the dead monk's tears he said, "Yes, indeed, it
is a very happy meeting," and he too wept.

The dead monk said, "You sit down here, hide yourself well
and peek through this hole in the wall to watch—oh, the pain
I endure. When I was at the temple I spent all my time simply
taking the offerings for the monks and eating them. On days I
felt lazy I would neither worship nor study. Because of those sins
I must suffer terrible, unendurable hardships one time a day. It
will be that time again soon." As he was speaking his expression
changed completely, becoming very pained and frightened. When
the living monk saw this he, too, felt an almost unendurable
fear.

The dead monk said, "Quickly, get into that room and hide,
and watch through the hole in the wall." The living monk followed these instructions and closed the door to peek through the
hole in the wall. Suddenly about forty or fifty Chinese-looking
people, extremely frightening, wearing headbands from the world
of the dead, came flying out of the sky. First they took crucifixes
of the type used to punish thieves and planted them quickly in
the earth. Then they made a big fire and put a large kettle over
it to heat up copper until it came to the consistency of water.
While this was going on three men who looked like bosses got
out folding chairs and put them down together, lining up several
red flags behind the chairs. Looking at this scene, the living
monk knew that it was not of this world.

Then the three called out in extremely fearsome voices, "Get them in here, quick!" and about twenty or thirty messengers went running about to the various monks' cells. Before long they all returned, dragging about ten monks by a scarlet rope. It looked like a chain gang. Among them were both acquaintances and strangers to the living monk.

All were brought to the base of the crucifixes and each was crucified. There was the same number of crucifixes as monks and so there were no crucifixes left over. None of the monks could move.

After putting them on the crucifixes the demons used large metal chopsticks to prop the monks' mouths open as wide as they would go. They shoved things resembling long metal funnels into the monks' open mouths and into these they poured the hot liquid copper, filling the mouths. In short order the copper passed through the monks' bodies and began to come out their buttocks. Flames were shooting from their eyes, ears and noses, and smoke was coming from all the joints of their bodies. All the monks were crying and yelling in pathetic voices. When the monks were all finished drinking the copper they were untied and led back to their rooms. Then the demons flew up into the sky and disappeared.

The living monk saw all this and although it was not of the living world, he panicked, wrapping himself up in his clothes, and lay cowering on his face.

In time the dead monk came in and opened the door. When the living monk got up and looked at him he saw that the dead monk had a very frightening look. The dead monk asked, "Did you see it?"

The living monk asked, "How long and for what reason have you been enduring such hardships?"

The dead monk replied, "Right after I died I came here and have been here since. Because I received offerings without working for them and never tried to atone for that sin I am receiving such punishments. Now leave quickly."

The living monk went out the door at these words and followed the road home. This time he easily found the temple. Afterwards he thought, "Buddha let me see that scene to show me that I too might receive such hardships," and faith rose in his heart. He did not take offerings from the temple again and confessed to taking earlier ones. It is reported that he became a most worthy holy man and served Buddha in a superior manner.

20:The Nobleman Who Married the Daughter of the Head Monk of Daian-ji. Long ago there was a person called [   ], who was the monk in charge of the temple Daian-ji. His daughter was a woman of beautiful appearance and a charming bearing. A nobleman called [   ] was visiting her secretly in the evenings. They felt very close to one another and were scarcely able to part, and so it was that there were even times when he stayed at her house all day without returning home.

Once when he had stayed on through the day and they were taking an afternoon nap the man had a dream. In his dream all the members of the household began weeping and making a big commotion.

He wondered, "What could be making people weep like this?" and got up to go look—everyone in the house, from his father-in-law the monk and his mother-in-law the nun, on down was carrying metal pots and weeping in confusion. Wondering, "Why are they carrying metal pots and weeping?" he looked even more closely and discovered that molten copper had been poured into all the pots.

And this liquid copper, which not even a demon could force a person to swallow—why, they were weeping with all their hearts and drinking it. Some of them, when they had finally finished drinking it, begged for more and drank that as well. Right down to the lowest servant in the house, there was no one who did not drink it.

A lady-in-waiting then came in to call the woman who was sleeping next to him on the bed. She arose and went in. As he looked on in disbelief a lady-in-waiting put some of the molten copper in a large silver cup and offered it to his wife, who took it and, crying out in a pathetic voice, drank it in tears. Flames and smoke came from her eyes, ears, and nose.

As he watched all this in bewilderment someone said, "Have the guest come in," and a lady-in-waiting put some of the molten copper in a cup which she then placed on a tray and brought in. At that time he realized in horror, "They are planning to make me drink some of this, too," and screaming and making a commotion he awoke from his dream.

He looked around with a start and saw that a lady-in-waiting had brought some food in on a tray. His father-in-law was also eating noisily. Then the man realized, "This man is the head monk of the temple but he is helping himself to the property of the temple and eating the property of the temple. This is what I saw in the dream."

He was repelled and lost all his interest in the woman. Thus, he decided, "I should not eat any of this at all," and saying that he did not feel well he left without saying any more. Later he still felt repelled and did not come back again.

After this the man felt particularly repentant. Although he did not feel so strongly as to take the vows, he had some faith, and it is said that he never misused the property of Buddha.

As a quick footnote to the second story, I would point out that the lacunae at the beginning of the tale are examples of what I have discussed above as intentional lacunae, which are fairly common in *Konjaku* in the case of proper nouns. Apparently the compiler intended to verify his information and fill in the blank spaces at a later time. It was customary for the man to visit his wife at the house of her parents, especially early in their marriage. If the woman were the chief wife the man would generally move with her into a separate house though this did not always happen. Men frequently had more than one wife.

Let us now consider these stories as literary creations, paying particular attention to the way they complement one another. To put them in their overall context, the first eighteen stories in volume XIX deal with the taking of the vows and becoming a Buddhist monk (or nun), and the next few tales in this volume are about the dangers of misusing Buddhist property. Thus there is an apparent break between stories 18 and 19, although it would be readily acknowledged that 19 and 20 go together to make a pair in the sense of Kunisaki's *ni wa, ichi rui* concept.

Story 19 is, however, connected to story 18 on various levels. One of these is the matter of religious resolve, which wells up in the hero when he sees the horrible punishment in store for him if he continues to use temple property for his own ends; religious resolve is a major theme in story 18. Another is that the two tales contrast Buddhist monks—the monks in story 19 are sinners, but in story 18 we have both Zōga and Genshin, who are portrayed as being very holy. Although the living monk in story 19 is already a monk and hence cannot take the vows, he does renew his vows. In much the same way the young aristocratic hero in story 20 pledges to lead a better life.

The links between stories 19 and 20 are obvious—both are about the misuse of Buddhist property and the punishment of drinking molten copper.

To illustrate the importance the compiler put on the links between his stories we might note that story 20 is thought to have come from the same source as *Uji Shūi Monogatari* 112, and the two tales are very close in wording and plot. The only major difference between them is the commentary, supplied by the *Konjaku* compiler but not present in *Uji Shūi:* "Although he did not feel so strongly as to take the vows he had some faith." The presence of this sentence adds the idea of religious resolve and faith to the tale and thus underscores the link between this tale in *Konjaku* and story 19.

There is also a less concrete linking between the two stories, and this provides the key to our critical understanding of the *Konjaku* compiler's literary consciousness. Both stories deal with the theme of illusion and reality (which, incidentally, is the most important theme treated in volume XIX), and the compiler uses his *ni wa, ichi rui* concept to make some rather subtle points in this respect.

In story 19 we have a Dantesque vision of punishments that fit the crime in the monks who are forced to drink molten copper after their deaths to atone for the sins of their lifetimes. This story apparently postulates a separation of the worlds of the living and of the dead, and while the fate of the dead may have been settled by what the person did while alive (the classic idea of cause and effect), the two worlds are nonetheless separate and distinct. The living monk hero who bridges the gap is said to be walking through the unknown mountains "as if in a dream," indicating that he has passed from one realm of existence to another. Parenthetically, it should be noted that the mountains were believed by the Heian Japanese to be one of the places where the souls of the dead went and hence a contemporary audience would have recognized this passage from one world to another. The point is that the world of the living is one realm and the world of the dead is a different realm in this story.

Story 20, however, adds a dimension to this idea of the separation of worlds. In this tale we see that when the monk's family consumes temple property in this world what it is *really* doing is drinking molten copper. If this is true, then it is the acts performed after death in story 19 that are real; that which we do in this life, it follows, must be illusion.

The apparent distinction between worlds in story 19 must now be reexamined, for the drinking of molten copper is not a punishment for having misused temple property, it is *equal* to misusing temple property. To clarify this even further we might point to story 21, in which a monk who makes *sake* from rice donated to his temple sees snakes in the *sake* container rather than liquid even though those innocent of his sins see *sake* inside the pots.

People are deluded by the illusions of the world and cannot recognize the fact that what they call reality in truth is an illusion. Therefore they continue to perform acts which are in reality destructive, and think that they are enjoying themselves in the process. The truth is only revealed when we enter those realms we normally consider to be unreal—dreams or death. This is more than simple cause and effect, for the truth is that one is not forced to drink molten copper after death *because* one consumed temple property in life; rather, one has been consuming molten copper all the time and enjoying it. We only become aware of the horror and the reality of our actions after death, or after we enter the world we would usually think of as illusory.

The fact that the monk in story 19 is wandering "as if in a dream" is thus important, for when taken together with story 20 and the dream shown there it tells us that the dream-death stage is the stage in which we learn the true nature of reality. The hero most often celebrated by the *Konjaku* compiler is the person who is able to understand the nature of truth when he encounters it.

Even though illusion might be more real than "reality" to the *Konjaku* compiler, he does not go so far as to deny the world of the senses altogether. After all, one of the reasons for the making of the collection was to teach people how to live correctly in this world. The compiler is concerned with teaching us how to recognize truth when we see it, and how to avoid being misled by the illusions foisted on us by our senses.

The compiler approaches this task on two basic levels. One of these is didactic and Buddhist, but the other is more literary. The forceful descriptions of people drinking molten copper appeal to the senses and are calculated to frighten some into compliance, but there is a more subtle probing into reality and illusion based on these thematic links between stories. If, for example, we were to read only story 19 we would not see the complete picture and would thus have an incomplete understanding of reality. It is the progressive movement of the tales which adds to our gradual understanding of the larger picture of reality being drawn by the compiler. One is reminded of Heian poetry and its method of contrasting the inner and outer realities experienced by the poet in order to suggest that illusion might be more real than that which we can apprehend with the senses. Direct statement is used by neither the poets nor the *Konjaku* compiler, for a direct statement would not allow the reader to come to his own understanding of the truth.

These two stories could be understood and analyzed on at least three different levels. First, they are interesting stories, likely to hold the attention of their readers or listeners because they deal with events which are out of the ordinary. We could, accordingly, examine their narrative structure and see how they present the material.

Second, they are rather simple didactic stories which show the terrible punishments awaiting those who misuse temple property. We could show other examples of such stories in Buddhism and begin to compile a list of Buddhist ideals from these tales and others like them.

Finally, they represent a literary effort to deal with the question of reality, for they show us that what we normally term illusion is in truth more real than reality, and that reality is not as easy to perceive as we might think. This they accomplish by suggestion rather than direct statement, and we could profitably compare them to a number of Japanese poems.

It might be noted that such a multi-leveled approach to the material is in keeping with the Buddhist idea of *hōben,* or accommodated truth. By presenting his material on different levels the compiler allows people with various levels of understanding to profit from what he has to say.

The stories are able to function on such different levels because of the nature of the *setsuwa,* which provides the compiler with a credible story; the Buddhist world view, which on a simple level condemns the sin of misusing Buddhist property and on a more complex level holds that nothing in this transitory world is real, that all is illusion; and finally because of the artistic editorial practices of the compiler, which allows for the association of images to make suggestions about reality. A large number of the stories in *Konjaku Monogatari-shū* can be approached as I have approached these two tales.[2]

Conclusion

The raw material of *Konjaku Monogatari-shū* is the *setsuwa* itself, a brief tale about some extraordinary event. We can, on the simplest of levels, understand and appreciate *Konjaku* as being a collection of such tales, a kind of smorgasbord for the lover of good stories. Seen in these terms *Konjaku* is not especially artistic, although it is in places very interesting if one happens to enjoy the kinds of stories the compiler has gathered.

These stories have been given a considerable amount of attention by the compiler, who had definite ideas on the best kind of narrative. Generally speaking, he strove for a maximum amount of action, and made liberal use of dialogue and internal monologue. His descriptions run to the vivid, with great concern for dramatizing the motives of the characters. Above all, the compiler worked to make the action of the individual tales more immediate to the reader.

But *Konjaku* is more than a collection of stories. It is a kind of guidebook to success in a chaotic world, and through its tales the compiler attempts both to illuminate the nature of the world he and his audience were forced to live in and to provide specific strategies for coping with the world as well. His answers are first of all Buddhist—one needs faith in the power of Buddhism for success—but they also involve cleverness and the ability to understand illusions for what they are. This stress on illusion and reality is one of the major factors which unites the Buddhist and secular stories, for it is a topic which transcends either Buddhist or non-Buddhist concerns.

Because Buddhist answers are the most valid to the compiler he also works to provide a thorough understanding of the nature of Buddhism to his audience. This he accomplishes through his historical background, tracing Buddhism from India, into China, and on to Japan; in addition, he spends considerable time demonstrating Buddhist ideas through his tales.

He transforms the raw *setsuwa* in his collection largely through his use of them. His "two tales, one type" method of arrangement of tales, for example, allows for expansion from the narrow concerns of the tales themselves to broader concerns held by the compiler himself.

The compiler of *Konjaku Monogatari-shū* was indeed a man with a vision, and he used the tales in his collection to make that vision apparent to his readers. Perhaps the greatest testimony to his skills as a narrator and as a poet is the fact that today, after more than eight hundred years have passed, both the stories and the vision continue to attract us. Surely this must be the final statement on the value of *Konjaku Monogatari-shū*.

Notes and References

Chapter One

1. A good discussion of the history of the late Heian period can be found in G. Cameron Hurst, "The Development of the *Insei:* A Problem in Japanese History and Historiography," in John W. Hall and Jeffrey P. Mass, eds., *Medieval Japan: Essays in Institutional History* (New Haven: Yale University Press, 1974), pp. 60–90.

2. Chief among these are the so-called *rokushōji,* which draw their names from the fact that each temple has the word *shō* in its name: Hosshō-ji (1072), Sonshō-ji (1102), Saishō-ji (1118), Enshō-ji (1128), Seishōji (1139), and another Enshō-ji (1149). All were built by retired emperors.

3. For a more detailed discussion see W. Michael Kelsey, "Didactics in Art: The Literary Structure of *Konjaku Monogatari-shū,*" (Diss., Indiana University, 1976), pp. 135–48.

4. See Murayama Shuichi, *Heian Kyō* (Tokyo: Seibundō 1966), especially pp. 117–18, for a more detailed discussion. Murayama notes that both ceremonies had specialists in chanting, judges, and so on.

5. *Hyaku-za Hōdan Kikigaki-shō* is described in more detail in Chapter 2.

6. See Chapter 2 for references to *setsuwa* in the diary *Chūyūki.*

7. See, for example, Robert H. Brower, "The Koñzyaku Monogatarisyū: An Historical and Critical Introduction, with Annotated Translations of Seventy-eight Tales," (Diss., University of Michigan, 1952), especially pp. 265–66.

8. Tamura Yoshirō, "The New Buddhism of Kamakura and Nichiren," *Acta Asiatica* 20 (1971):46.

9. A complete translation of this preface can be found in D. E. Mills, trans., *A Collection of Tales from Uji* (Cambridge, 1970), p. 83. The translation here is taken from Watanabe Tsunaya and Nishio Kōichi, eds., *Uji Shūi Monogatari* (Tokyo: Iwanami Shoten, 1960), pp. 48–49.

10. Katayose Masayoshi, *Konjaku Monogatari-shū no Kenkyū* (Tokyo, 1974), I, 9. Mills summarizes the problem on pp. 99–103.

11. I do not mean to imply that Takakuni was ignorant of Buddhism, or that he has been discounted by all modern scholars. He is known to have been the editor of a ten-volume work called *An'yō-shū*, which was a learned work on the Pure Land that supposedly drew from a large number of written sources. There is, however, no direct evidence to link him with *Konjaku*.

12. Katayose, I, 112–31.

13. Sakai's thesis is outlined in his article "Ban Nobutomo Suzuka-bon Konjaku Monogatari-shū Kenkyū ni Michibikarete," *Kokugo-Kokubun*, October 1975, pp. 23–29.

14. See Hirabayashi Shigetoku, "Konjaku Monogatari-shū Gembon no Tōdaiji Sonzai Setsu ni Tsuite," *Nihon Rekishi*, January 1978, pp. 1–29.

15. Takahashi Mitsugu, *Chūko Setsuwa Bungaku Kenkyū Josetsu* (Tokyo, 1974), p. 243.

Chapter Two

1. The quotations from *Chūyūki* are taken from volume V of *Chūyūki* in Tōkyō Daigaku Shiryō Hensan, ed., *Dai-Nihon Shiryō Taisei* (Tokyo: Tokyo University Press, 1935); the diary is arranged in chronological order and I have not supplied page numbers.

2. See, for example, Linda Degh, "The Belief Legend in Modern Society," in Wayland D. Hand, ed., *American Folk Legend: A Symposium* (Berkeley: University of California Press, 1971), pp. 55–68. Degh and other folklorists have written extensively on this topic.

3. See, for example, D. E. Mills, *A Collection of Tales from Uji*, p. 3.

4. Endo Yoshimoto and Kasuga Kazuo, eds., *Nihon Ryōiki* (Tokyo: Iwanami Shoten, 1967), p. 54. An English translation of this work has been made by Kyoko Motomochi Nakamura: *Miraculous Stories from the Japanese Buddhist Tradition: The Nihon Ryōiki of the Monk Kyōkai* (Cambridge, Mass.: Harvard University Press, 1973).

5. For a discussion of the role of the *shamon* in the development of *Ryōiki* see Kurosawa Kōzō, *Nihon Kodai Denshō Bungaku no Kenkyū* (Tokyo, 1976), p. 265.

6. I must acknowledge my debt to Kurosawa for much of the following material. See in particular *Nihon Kodai Denshō Bungaku no Kenkyū*, pp. 154–222.

7. W. G. Aston, trans., *Nihongi, Chronicles of Japan from the Earliest Times to* A.D. 697 (Rutland, Vt., and Tokyo: Charles Tuttle, 1972), I, 347.

8. There is an English translation of this tale in Nakamura, *Miraculous Stories,* pp. 102–104.

9. Yanagita Kunio makes the connection between stories such as "Issun Bōshi" and the tales of the thunder deity and small children in his *Monogatari to Katarimono,* in *Teihon Yanagita Kunio Shū* (Tokyo: Chikuma Shobō, 1968), pp. 5–19. See in particular p. 8.

10. Kurosawa, p. 205.

11. In the Nō play *Dōjō-ji,* for example, we have the tale of how an angry woman has transformed herself into a snake-deity and wrapped herself around a temple bell in which a monk who refused her advances is hiding; since that incident the temple has been without a bell. There are other such examples.

12. Katharine Briggs, *An Encyclopedia of Fairies, Hobgoblins, Brownies, Bogies, and Other Supernatural Creatures* (New York: Pantheon Books, 1976), p. 57.

13. Joseph Fontenrose, *Python: A Study of Delphic Myth and Its Origins* (Berkeley: University of California Press, 1959), p. 57.

14. In the *Kojiki* this tale is used to explain the birth of Opo Tata Neko as the offspring of the Mt. Miwa deity.

15. See the article by Seiki Keigo ("The Spool of Thread: A Subtype of the Japanese Serpent Bridegroom Tale") in Richard M. Dorson, ed., *Studies in Japanese Folklore* (Port Washington, N.Y.: Indiana University Press, 1959), pp. 267–88.

16. It should be noted that snakes and dragons are interchangeable in folklore. See Briggs, *An Encyclopedia,* under "dragon." Another *Konjaku* tale on this general topic, incidentally, is XXXI.34; in this story a deity takes the form of a snake during the daytime and his mortal lover is repulsed and rejects him, so he kills her. This story has a parallel in *Nihon Shoki.* I have dealt extensively with such tales in "Salvation of the Snake, the Snake of Salvation: Buddhist-Shinto Conflict and Resolution," *Japanese Journal of Religious Studies,* 8/1–2 (1981):83–113.

17. An example of this tale, known in Japanese as "Tennin Nyobō," can be found in English as "The Woman Who Came Down from Heaven," in Seiki Keigo, ed., *Folktales of Japan* (Chicago: University of Chicago Press, 1963), pp. 63–69.

18. In the tale cited above, for example, the woman drops one of her children on her ascent to Heaven. This child is fed magically for a time, but when a woman washes something dirty in the stream which is the source of the child's food—thus polluting it—the supply shrinks to almost nothing and the child disappears. See Ibid., p. 69.

19. It is possible, of course, that someone other than the *Konjaku* compiler gave the Kume tale its present form. There are three other written versions of this tale extant; however, the only one which probably predates *Konjaku* (found in *Fusō Ryakki*, compiled in 1094), has very few similarities to the *Konjaku* version.

20. See Mills, pp. 5–22, for a survey of the major collections.

21. Quoted in Satō Kenzō, *Heian Jidai Bungaku no Kenkyū* (Tokyo: Kadokawa Shoten, 1960), p. 163.

22. The figures come from Yamada, *Konjaku*, Vol. III.

23. Nakajima Etsuji, ed., *Uchigiki-shū* (Tokyo: Hakutei-sha, 1961), pp. 12–13.

24. See Mills, pp. 17–18.

25. *Yamato Monogatari* (c. 950), in particular, is of note as a collection of stories intended for entertainment.

26. Kawaguchi Hisao, ed., *Kohon Setsuwa-shū* (Tokyo: Asahi Shimbun-sha, 1967), p. 17.

27. The most common figure offered is seven, and not eight; I add XIX.10 as a variant of *Hosshin-shū* 54.

28. Takahashi Mitsugu, *Chūko Setsuwa Bungaku*, says there are seventeen such stories, while Mills finds twenty-two. Takahashi, p. 129; Mills, pp. 442–45 (Table 5).

29. I have arbitrarily arranged the tales in the order in which they appear in *Konjaku*. Stories in *USM* and *KHS* are arranged consecutively, with no volume numbers, so to read the table simply read across, with the numbers in the horizontal columns representing the story number in each collection of that collection's version of one given tale.

30. Takahashi, pp. 130–31; Mills, pp. 69–71.

31. Takahashi, pp. 130–35.

32. Ibid., p. 138.

33. Mills, p. 13.

34. Takahashi, p. 137.

35. Ibid., pp. 137–38.

36. Mills, p. 72.

37. Ibid., p. 73.

Chapter Three

1. See Kunisaki Fumimaro, *Konjaku Monogatari-shū Seiritsu Kō* (Tokyo, 1962), pp. 171–77, for a summary of Kunisaki's ideas. The chart between pages 120 and 121 is also helpful.

2. See Yamada Yoshio et al., eds., *Konjaku Monogatari-shū* (Tokyo, 1959–1963), I, 360. Although this tale bears many resemblances to *Jātaka* stories, it is not contained in *Jātaka Stories*, Pali Texts Society, ed. (Cambridge: Cambridge University Press, 1895), in six volumes.

3. Wu Ch'eng-en, *Monkey, Folk Novel of China*, trans. Arthur Waley (New York: Grove Press, 1943). Waley's translation is an abridgement of the original; a translation being published by Anthony Yu through the University of Chicago Press, three volumes of which have appeared at this writing, will present the novel in full.

4. This is the opinion of Yamada. See Yamada, *Konjaku*, II, 65.

5. For a translation of the poem see Cyril Birch, ed., *Anthology of Chinese Literature* (New York: Grove Press, 1965), I, 266–77. Po Chü-yi was an extremely popular poet in Japan and it is safe to assume that his work was known by all members of the aristocracy.

6. Also read Gyōgi.

7. He is also known as En no Gyōja, E no Gyōja, and by various other names as well.

8. See Chapter 2 for a discussion of the *ōjō den*.

9. I find it interesting that Jizō is portrayed as a child with extraordinary power; we have seen in Chapter 2 that small size and great power are traits associated with the offspring of the thunder deity, who is a Shinto, not a Buddhist, figure.

10. A complete translation of this story is included in Chapter 5.

11. See Nagano Jōichi, ed., *Konjaku Monogatari* (Tokyo, 1953), I, 118.

12. I have generally followed the identification of sources for the various *Konjaku* tales as cited in the Yamada edition; this is more recent than the Haga *Kōshō Konjaku Monogatari-shū*, which contains the complete texts of all sources identified by Haga. Haga's text has been the source for all translations from Chinese works in this and other chapters. Yamada identifies the sources of the stories both in the table of contents of each volume and in a general footnote before each tale.

13. See Chapter 5 for a more detailed discussion of how this is accomplished.

14. Katayose, I, 454.

15. Ibid., p. 474.

16. See Kawaguchi Hisao, "*Konjaku Monogatari-shū to Kohon Setsuwa Shū* ni tsuite," p. 64.

17. Ibid.

18. Kikuchi Ryōichi, "Konjaku Monogatari ni Okeru Bukkyō Sezokuka ni tsuite," *Nihon Bungaku* 30 (January, 1954):28.

19. Kunisaki, *Seiritsu Kō,* especially pp. 38–46. For an English discussion of many of the Chinese *setsuwa* collections which had influence on *Konjaku* see Donald E. Gjertson, "A Study and Translation of the *Ming-Pao Chi:* A Tang Dynasty Collection of Buddhist Tales," Unpublished Diss. Stanford, 1975.

20. Ishigaki Kenji, "Goho yori Mitaru *Konjaku Monogatari,*" *Kokugo to Kokubungaku* 18 (November, 1941). Quoted in Nishio Kōichi, *"Konjaku Monogatari-shū* Kenkyū Shi," p. 56. Nishio does not accept Ishigaki's conclusions.

21. See W. Michael Kelsey, "Didactics in Art: The Literary Structure of *Konjaku Monogatari-shū,*" pp. 61–67, for a more complete summary of scholarship in this area.

22. Ibid., especially p. 66.

Chapter Four

1. See Mitani Eiichi, *Monogatari Bungaku-shi Ron* (Tokyo: Yūseidō, 1962), especially pp. 10–20. I am indebted for much of what follows to Mitani's ideas, as expressed in this book and in "Tsukuri Monogatari to Setsuwa," in Kunisaki Fumimaro and Kanda Hideo, eds., *Nihon no Setsuwa,* Vol. II, pp. 160–85.

2. See Chapter 5 for a more thorough discussion.

3. This tale was discussed briefly in Chapter 2.

4. Konishi Jin'ichi, "Association and Progression: Principles of Integration in Anthologies and Sequences of Japanese Court Poetry, A.D. 900–1350," *Harvard Journal of Asiatic Studies* 21 (1958): 67–127.

5. Kunisaki Fumimaro, *Konjaku Monogatari-shū Seiritsu Kō,* pp. 1–8.

6. In "Didactics in Art," I have shown how these principles apply in the study of an entire volume (XIX). The Yamada edition of *Konjaku,* it should be pointed out, makes note of the links between stories in each of the volumes of the collection, though incompletely.

7. Kunisaki, p. 44.

8. These were the authors of the diary *Kagerō Nikki* and the *setsuwa* collection *Sambō E Kotoba.*

9. Ōtsu Yūichi and Chikushima Hazama, eds.; *Ise Monogatari* (Tokyo: Iwanami Shoten, 1957), pp. 150–52. For a discussion of *Ise,* Narihira, and the poetry of the collection, see Helen Craig McCullough, trans., *Tales of Ise: Lyrical Episodes from Tenth-Century Japan* (Stanford: Stanford University Press, 1968), especially pp. 55–65.

10. Ibid., p. 230 (note 3 to episode 69).

11. These are *Konjaku* XXIV.35 (*Ise* 9), XXIV.36 (*Ise* 99), and XXX.4 (*Ise* 62). There are also tales in *Konjaku* XXX with parallels in *Yamato Monogatari* and *Heichū Monogatari*, both of which are often considered poem-tale collections. A more thorough discussion of the topic can be found in Kobayashi Hiroko, *The Human Comedy of Heian Japan* (Tokyo, 1979).

12. Mitani Eiichi, *Monogatari*, pp. 21–23.

13. Ibid., pp. 23–24.

14. See Yanagita Kunio's article on *Taketori* and the Taketori legends in *Mukashi Banashi to Bungaku* (Tokyo: Chikuma Shobō, 1963). Yanagita says that the most important motif in this story is that of the feather robe (*hagoromo*). In many of the oral versions of this tale the woman is unable to return home without the robe and must search for it, but in *Taketori* she has been exiled from her home, and when she once again dons the robe she forgets her experiences as a human.

15. See Mitani Eiichi, "Tsukuri Monogatari," pp. 161–62.

16. See, for example, D. E. Mills, "*Soga Monogatari, Shintōshū* and the Taketori Legend," *Monumenta Nipponica* 30 (Spring 1975):37–68. Mills lists eighteen different works in which the story appears.

17. Kikuchi Ryōichi, "Konjaku Monogatari ni Okeru Bukkyō Sezoku-ka ni tsuite," *Nihon Bungaku* 30 (January 1954):28.

18. For a survey of the textual families in Heike studies see Kenneth D. Butler, "The Textual Evolution of the Heike Monogatari," *Harvard Journal of Asiastic Studies* 26 (1966):36–75.

19. *Konjaku* XXV.1. The source for this story, incidentally, is the first extant Japanese war tale, *Shōmonki* (c. 940); the passage is identical in both works.

20. Ichiko Teiji, *Chūsei Shōsetsu no Kenkyū* (Tokyo: Iwanam; 1955), especially pp. 2–24.

21. Akutagawa Ryūnosuke, "Konjaku Monogatari Kanshō," in *Nihon Bungaku Kōza* (Tokyo: 1927). This is one of the most perceptive commentaries on *Konjaku* ever written.

Chapter Five

1. Mabuchi Kazuo, "Konjaku Monogatari-shū ni Okeru Ketsubun no Kenkyū," *Kokugo-Kokubun*, December 1948, pp. 173–185.

2. In "Didactics in Art" (pp. 174–291) I have analyzed all of the tales in volume XIX in such terms.

Selected Bibliography

PRIMARY SOURCES

1. In Japanese

The following editions of *Konjaku Monogatari-shū* are listed in alphabetical order by editor. All were published in Tokyo.

Haga, Yaichi. *Kōshō Konjaku Monogatari-shū.* Three volumes. Fuzanbō, 1913–1921. Also contains variants of all the tales known to Haga.

Mabuchi, Kazuo; Kunisaki, Fumimaro; and Konno, Tōru. *Konjaku Monogatari-shū.* Four volumes. Shōgaku-kan, 1971–1976. Contains good annotations and modern Japanese translations for all of the stories in the Japanese volumes (XI–XXXI).

Nagano, Jōichi. *Konjaku Monogatari.* Six volumes. Asahi Shimbun-sha, 1953–1957.

Yamada, Yoshio, et al. *Konjaku Monogatari-shū.* Five volumes. Iwanami Shoten, 1959–1963. Volumes 22–26 of the Nihon Koten Bungaku Taikei series.

2. In Western Languages

Following is a partial list of translations of various tales from *Konjaku* available in Western languages.

Brower, Robert H. "The *Koñzyaku Monogatarisyū:* An Historical and Critical Introduction, with Annotated Translations of Seventy-eight Tales." Diss. University of Michigan, 1952. Translations are from the Japanese stories, with summaries of tales from the earlier volumes.

Frank, Bernard. *Histoires qui sont maintenant du passé.* Paris: Gallimard, 1968. Includes an extensive introduction to the collection.

Jones, S. W. *Ages Ago—Thirty-seven Tales from the Konjaku Monogatari Collection.* Cambridge, Mass.: Harvard University Press, 1959. Does not include any of the Japanese Buddhist stories (Volumes XI–XX). Many of the translations are inaccurate.

Kelsey, W. Michael. "Didactics in Art: The Literary Structure of *Konjaku Monogatari-shū.*" Diss. Indiana University, 1976. Translations of all tales in volume XIX.

Schuster, Ingrid, and Müller, Klaus. *Erzählungen des alten Japan—aus dem Konjaku Monogatari.* Stuttgart: Philipp Reclam, 1965.

Tsukakoshi, Satoshi. *Konjaku: Altjapanische Geschicten aus dem Volk zur Heian-zeit.* Zurich: Max Niehans, 1956.

Ury, Marian. *Tales of Times Now Past: Sixty-two Stories from a Medieval Japanese Collection.* Berkeley and Los Angeles: University of California Press, 1979. Good selection, excellent translations.

Wilson, William R. "The Way of the Bow and Arrow: The Japanese Warrior in *Konjaku Monogatari.*" *Monumenta Nipponica* 28 (1973):177–233. Translations of all tales in volume XXV.

SECONDARY SOURCES

The following list is extremely selective. I have included works which I think are important for background as well as major studies of *Konjaku Monogatari-shū.*

Akutagawa, Ryūnosuke. "Konjaku Monogatari Kanshō." In *Nihon Bungaku Kōza,* VI. Tokyo: Shinchō-sha, 1927. Perceptive comments on the literary nature of the collection.

Hirabayashi, Shigetoku. "Konjaku Monogatari-shū Gembon no Tōdai-ji Zonzai Setsu ni Tsuite." *Nihon Rekishi,* January, 1978, pp. 1–29. A refutation of the theories of Sakai Kenji as to the authorship of *Konjaku.*

Katayose, Masayoshi. *Konjaku Monogatari-shū no Kenkyū.* Two volumes. Tokyo: Geirin-sha, 1974 (reprint of 1948 edition). An indispensable study of *Konjaku,* its sources, and its character.

————. *Konjaku Monogatari-shū Ron.* Tokyo: Geirin-sha, 1974 (reprint). A continuation of the above.

Kawaguchi, Hisao. "*Konjaku Monogatari-shū* to *Kohon Setsuwa-shū* ni Tsuite." In Nihon Bungaku Kenkyū Shiryō Hankō Kai, ed. *Konjaku Monogatari-shū* (see below), pp. 60–81. A comparison of the two works, containing important speculations as to the authorship of *Konjaku* and its function.

Kobayashi, Hiroko. *The Human Comedy of Heian Japan. A Study of the Secular Stories in the Twelfth-Century Collection of Tales, Konjaku Monogatarishū.* Tokyo: The Centre for East Asian Cultural Studies,

East Asian Cultural Series, No. 19, 1979. Pays particular attention to the types of characters appearing in volumes XXI to XXXI.

Kunisaki, Fumimaro. *Konjaku Monogatari-shū Seiritsu Kō.* Tokyo: Waseda University Press, 1962. A collection of Kunisaki's most important essays on *Konjaku,* including his theories on the collection's organization.

Kurosawa, Kōzō. *Nihon Kodai Denshō Bungaku no Kenkyū.* Tokyo: Hanawa Shobō, 1976. Stimulating essays on the origins of Japanese myth and the use of myth by early *setsuwa* collectors.

Mabuchi, Kazuo. *"Konjaku Monogatari-shū* ni Okeru Ketsubun no Kenkyū." *Kokugo-Kobubun,* December, 1948. pp. 173–85. Speculations on the reasons for lacunae in *Konjaku.*

Masuda, Katsumi. *Setsuwa Bungaku to Emaki.* Tokyo: San'ichi Shobō, 1960. Especially valuable for its comments on the origin of the *setsuwa* genre.

✓ Mills, D. E., trans. *A Collection of Tales from Uji.* Cambridge, Eng.: Cambridge University Press, 1970. A complete translation of *Uji Shūi Monogatari,* with a valuable introduction to the history of *setsuwa* literature and descriptions of the major *setsuwa* collections.

Nagano, Jōichi, ed. *Setsuwa Bungaku Jiten.* Tokyo: Tokyo-dō Shuppan, 1969. A valuable reference work, with a preface by Nagano and a good bibliography, including a section devoted to *Konjaku.*

Nihon Bungaku Kenkyū Shiryō Hankō Kai, ed. *Konjaku Monogatari-shū.* Tokyo: Yūseidō, 1970. Contains reprints of many important journal articles on *Konjaku* which might be otherwise difficult to obtain.

Nishio, Kōichi. *Chūsei Setsuwa Bungaku Ron.* Tokyo: Hanawa Shobō, 1963. A good survey of the *setsuwa* genre in the medieval period.

————. *"Konjaku Monogatari* Kenkyū Shi." *Kokubungaku: Kaishaku to Kanshō,* June 1959, pp. 51–63. A brief history of the research on *Konjaku,* especially convenient because it presents summaries of the leading scholarly opinions.

Sakai, Kenji. Ban Nobutomo Suzuka-bon *Konjaku Monogatari-shū* Kenkyū ni Michibikarete." *Kokugo-Kokubun,* October, 1975, pp. 23–29. A study based on manuscript notations, concluding that *Konjaku* was compiled by a monk at the Nara temple Tōdai-ji.

Sakai, Kōhei. *Konjaku Monogatari-shū no Shin-Kenkyū.* Tokyo: Meichō Hankō Kai, 1965 (special reprint of the 1923 edition). A pioneering study of the collection.

Takahashi, Mitsugu. *Chūko Setsuwa Bungaku Kenkyū Josetsu.* Tokyo: Ōfusha, 1974. Contains many sections on *Konjaku* and its relationship to other *setsuwa* collections. Takahashi holds that *Konjaku* was compiled by a monk or monks at the Tendai Buddhist Mt. Hiei headquarters.

Index

Akutagawa, Ryūnosuke,
  133–38, 139
Amida, 58, 59, 75, *80*
An Lu Shang rebellion, 72
Ariwara Narihira, *111–12,* 113,
  114
Aware, 119, 130, 137

Ban Nobutomo, 14
Belief legends, *22,* 124
Biwa hōshi, 127–28, 138
Bodhisattva worship, 81
Buddha image saves man from
  death, 66
Buddhist vows, taking of, 82,
  152–53

Chiisakobe no Sugaru, *25–26,*
  27
Chinese tales in *Konjaku
  Monogatari-shū,* 58, 59,
  64–73, 92–94
Ching-lü I-hsiang, 93
Chūyūki (Fujiwara Munetada), 6,
  20–21, 110

Daian-ji, 37, 151
Dai-Nihon Hokke Genki
  (Chingen), 35, *36–37,* 94

Diary, poetic, 103, *109–11;*
  preliterary, 109–10
Dōjō, priest, 27, *28*
Dragon. *See* serpent

Eiga Monogatari, 119
Eshin. *See* Genshin
En no Ubasoku, 78, 79
Enryaku-ji, 6, *15*

Fa-yüan Chu-lin, 95–96
Filial piety, *70–71,* 77, 82
Folk religion, 27
Fox transformations, *90–91,*
  106
Fugen, 76
Fujiwara, family, *3–4,* 83, 119,
  122
Fusō Ryakki, 162n19

Gangō-ji, 27
Genji Monogatari, 40, 56, 121,
  124, 133, 134, *139*
Genshin, 13, 17, 153
Go-Sanjō, Emperor, 4
Go-Shirakawa, Emperor, 4
Goshūi-shū, 118
Gunki. See War tales
Gyōki, 78–79

Hayashi, Michiharu, 11
Heian period, Buddhism in,
    4–10, 80, 125; literature of,
    102–125, 137, 138; social
    structure of, 3–4
Heichū Monogatari, 109
Heiji Monogatari, 126
Heike Monogatari, 125–26,
    126–30, 133, 137
Hijiri, 10
Hirabayashi, Shigetoku, 14–15
Hiragana, 56
Hōben, 9, 156
Hōgen Monogatari, 126, 127
Hojō-ji (Fujiwara Michinaga), 6
Hojō-ji (Fujiwara Tadahira), 5
Hōjōki (Kamo Chōmei), 126
Hosshin-shū (Kamo Chōmei), 41,
    44, 45
Hsi Yü Chi, 68, 69
Hsüan tsang, 68–70
Humor, 87, 88, 89, 122–23
Hung-Tsan Fa-hua Ch'uan, 13,
    95
Hyakuza Hōdan Kikigaki-shō, 7,
    35, 37–39

Ichiko Teiji, 131
Ima Kagami, 119
Indian tales in *Konjaku
    Monogatari-shū*, 58, 59,
    60–64, 92–94, 134
Insei, 4
Ise Monogatari, 101, 111–16,
    118, 125; episodes cited: 62,
    115; 69, 112–13
Issun bōshi, 28
Izumi Shikibu Nikki, 109

Japanese tales in *Konjaku
    Monogatari-shū*, general, 58,

59, 73–91, 94–95, 134;
    Buddhist, 73–83, 134;
    secular, 83–91, 134
Jātaka, 61, 63
Jinyō, 29
Jizō, Bodhisattva, 79, 81

Kagerō Nikki, 100
Kakujū. See *Konjaku Monogatari-
    shū*, compiler, Tōdai-ji theory
Kamakura period, Buddhism, 4,
    80, 125; literature, 125–26
Kankyo no Tomo, 44
Kannon, 47–48, 59, 65, 69,
    81, 105
Katakana, 56
Katayose, Masayoshi, 13,
    94–95, 96
Kawaguchi, Hisao, 95, 96
Kechien, 44
Keizen, 20–21
Ki Tsurayuki, 104–105, 107
Kiso Yoshinaka, 129
Kohon Setsuwa-shū, 40–41, 45;
    tales cited: 40, 47–49
    49–50; 69,
Kojiki, 24, 30
Kokin Waka-shū, 102, 104, 107,
    112, 117–18
Kokon Chomonjū, 120
Konjaku, meaning of, 55
Konjaku Monogatari-shū, audience
    of, 8, 108, 133, 154;
    compiler, Hieizan theory,
    15–16, 17; compiler, Tōdai-ji
    theory, 13–15; compiler,
    traditional theory, 11–13;
    editorial method, 108, 140,
    148, 153–56, 157; language
    of, 56, 97; narrative style of,

50, 93, 137–38, 140,
  141–47, organization by
  geography, 2, 56,–57;
  organization by subject
  matter, 57 sources for,
  91–98; See also Tales cited
  from
Kotobagaki, 101
Kūkai, 5
Kume no Sennin, 32–33
Kunisaki Fumimaro, 57, 63,
  64–65, 74, 84–85, 96–97,
  108
Kurosawa, Akira, 134, 135
Kuan Yin. See Kannon.

Lacunae in Konjaku Monogatari-
  shū, 141, 152
Legends. See Belief legends
Lotus Sutra, 5, 10, 29, 36–37,
  58, 59, 67, 75–78, 79–80,
  140

Mappō, 9, 21, 58, 140
Miidera, 15, 20, 21
Mills, D.E., 34, 51, 52
Minamoto, Takakuni. See
  Konjaku Monogatari-shū,
  compiler, traditional theory
Minamoto, Yoritomo, 125,
  126–27
Minamoto, Yoshitsune, 127
Minamoto family, 126–27
Ming-pao Chi, 96
Mitani, Eiichi, 101–102, 114,
  122
Miwa, Mountain, 30
Mizu Kagami, 119
Molten copper, drinking of,
  150, 151, 153, 154–55

Monkey. See Hsi Yü Chi
Mongatari, meaning of,
  101–102, 114
Monogatari genres, 111–24
Monokusa Tarō, 131–32
Morals, in Konjaku Monogatari-
  shū tales, 93–94, 136, 144,
  153
Mujō, 127, 130, 137
Mumyō Zōshi, 100

Narrative distance, 133, 134,
  136
Ni wa, ichi rui. See Knojaku
  Monogatari-shū, editorial
  method
Nihon Ōjō Gokuraku-ki
  (Yoshishige Yasutani), 41, 42,
  45, 94
Nihon Ryōiki (Kyōkai), 23–29,
  35, 37, 94, 97; preface, 23;
  tales cited from: I.1, 25–26;
  I.3, 26–28; I.7, 143–46;
  II.41, 31; III.14, 24
Nihon Shoki, 24, 25, 26
Nikki. See Diary
Nō drama, 126, 130–31

Ochikubo Monogatari, 121, 124
Oda Maki, story cycle of, 32
Ōjō den, 42, 44, 45, 80
Ōkagami, 40, 119, 120
Ono Takamura, 117–18
Otogizōshi, 126, 131–33

Pathos. See aware
Performance literature, 132–33,
  137–38
Pheasant monk, story of, 20–21

Poem tales, 40, 101, *111–19*, 128

Poetry. *See tanka*

Preaching, 7, 35, 39, 53–54, 96, 133, 138, 155, 156

Proficiency, as theme in *Konjaku Monogatari-shū*, 87, 88

Progression and integration in poetry collections, 107

Pure Land. *See* Western Paradise

Pure Land Buddhism, 9–10

Rashōmon, film version, 134, *135*

Reality and illusion, as theme in *Konjaku Monogatari-shū*, 105–106, 135, 153, *154–56*, 157

Rekishi monogatari, 119–20

Retribution, *71*, 82

Romance. *See Tsukuri monogatari*

Ryōgen, 15

Saichō, 5

Saigyō, 43

Sakai, Kenji, 140

Sake becomes snakes, motif of, 154

Sanbō E Kotaba (Minamoto Tamenori), *35–36*, 100, 121

San-pao Kan-ying Yao Lüeh-lu, 96–97, 142

Sarashina Nikki, 110

Self-sacrifice, as theme in *Konjaku Monogatari-shū*, 61, 66, 70, 73

Senjūshō, 41, 43

Sericulture, 31

Serpents, 22, *25–27*, 30–31, 101, 161n16; raping women, 31, 32, 89

Setsuwa, 1, *18–34;* and myth, 23–32; and folktales, 32–34; and literature, 99–102; characteristics of, 19; transmission of, 21

Setsuwa collections, classification of, 35

Shamon, 23, *24–25*

Shingon Buddhism, 5

Shinto, conflict with Buddhism, 28, *29*

Shirakawa, Emperor, 4

Shōbō, 57

Shōtoku, Prince Regent, 78

Small children, *27*, 76, 81, 163n9

Song of Everlasting Sorrow, the (Po Chü-yi), 72

Stupidity, as theme in *Konjaku Monogatari-shū*, 87, 89, 135

Sujin, Emperor, 30

Sun Goddess, 43

Sutras, stories in praise of, 67, 79

Taiheiki, 126

Taira, Kiyomori, 4, *127*

Taira, Masakado, 129

Taira family, 126, 127

Takahashi, Mitsugu, 15–16, 51, 52, 53

Takamura Monogatari, 109, 121

Taketori Monogatari, 121–24

Tales cited from *Konjaku Monogatari-shū*, III.14, 16; IV.24, 51; IV.37, 38–39; V.8, *60–61*, 62, 92–93; V.31, 52; VI.1, 52; VI.6, 68–70; VI.11, *65–66*, 142; VII.3, 93; VII.21, 67; IX.7,

70; IX.13, 52–53; IX.17,
71; X.7, 72; X.9, 72–73;
X.13, 73; XI.2, 78–79;
XI.11, 52; XI.24, 32–33;
XII.1, 29; XII.29, 80;
XVI.8, 81; XVI.19, 81;
XIX.3, 42; XIX.5, 116;
XIX.10, 146–47; XIX.11,
47–49, 105–106; XIX.13,
49–50; XIX.15, 82; XIX.19,
82, 148–51; XIX.20,
151–51; XIX.30, 143–46;
XX.3, 106; XX.10, 82–83;
XXIV.5, 85–87; XXIV.9,
32; XXIV.23, 88; XXIV.45,
117–18; XXV.1, 129;
XXV.3, 130; XXV.4, 130;
XXV.12, 88; XXVI.2,
89–90; XXVII.41, 90–91;
XXVIII.3, 120; XXVIII.24,
89; XXIX.18, 89; XXIX.23,
134–35; XXIX.39, 89;
XXIX.40, 22; XXX.4,
115–16; XXXI.33, 123–24;
XXXI.34, 161n16
Tanka, 102, 103–109, 126,
155
Temple bells and snakes, 27,
28, 161n11
Tendai Buddhism, 5, 9
Tengu, 106
Tennin nyobō, tale cycle, 33,
122, 161n17
Thunder deity. See serpents

Tōdai-ji, 13–15, 79, 148
Tsukuri-monogatari, 100, 103,
120–24

Uchigiki-shū, 35, 39–40, 45;
tales cited from: 2, 52; 18,
52; 20, 52; 21, 52–53
Uji Dainagon Monogatari
(Minamoto Takakuni), 11–12,
94
Uji Shūi Monogatari, 41, 45,
133, 136; preface to, 11; tales
cited from, 42, 8; 89, 47–49;
112, 153; 164, 52–53; 170,
52; 171, 52; 195, 52
Underworld, visit to, 65–66,
77, 81, 142, 148–51
Unidentified flying objects,
stories concerning, 22
Upāya. See hōben
Uta monogatari. See poem tales
Utsubo Monogatari, 121, 124

Waley, Arthur, 68
War tales, genre, 125–30; in
Konjaku Monogatari-shū, 88,
128–30
Western Paradise, rebirth in,
21, 36, 38–39, 42, 79,
80–81, 82, 140

Yamato Monogatari, 116, 118
Yōen, 8

Zōbō, 57, 71
Zōga, holy man, 43, 153